PROPHETS and PROPHECY

Prophets and Prophecy

SEVEN KEY MESSENGERS

FRANK H. SEILHAMER

FORTRESS PRESS   Philadelphia

Library of Congress Catalog Card Number 76-62603
ISBN 0-8006-1254-X

6180J76   Printed in U.S.A.   1-1254

TO
Lutheran Theological Seminary
Gettysburg, Pennsylvania
and
Dropsie University
Philadelphia, Pennsylvania
where the teachings and compassion of the
prophets were first brought alive for me

CONTENTS

Preface   ix

1. Prophecy—"The Word of the Lord Came . . ."   1

2. Moses: Covenant   8

3. Isaiah: Sin and Restoration   18

4. Hosea: Forgiveness   30

5. Amos: Judgment, Justice, and Renewal   41

6. Micah: Righteousness and Obedience   50

7. Jeremiah: Salvation and Faithfulness   59

8. Ezekiel: Punishment and Resurrection   70

9. The Prophets for Today   78

For Further Reading   84

PREFACE

The basic material contained in this book first appeared in shorter form as a series of articles published in *The Lutheran*. While the original subjects were addressed to a general audience, it was essentially for laypersons that I wrote then as I have done in the preparation of this book. This is not to say that the material contained between these covers is of no interest or value to pastors, teachers, or other students of the Scriptures. The fact is that my primary interest was to introduce to these great "spokesmen for the Lord" those who may not have been familiar with the biblical prophets and their messages before. In that encounter, hopefully, such individuals might be caught up and enlivened through meeting these sensitive and perceptive spiritual pilgrims of old who might then become their lifelong friends.

Over the last thirty years these earthy, wise, and honest teachers of faith and ways of living have become my intimate partners and counselors. They have challenged me, supported me, warned me, and shaped me in all areas of my life more than I will ever know. As I have lived out my life with its joys, struggles, anxieties, and at times moments of despair, these giants of the past have hung in with me and helped me stay aware of the powerful presence of God, enabling me to grow personally and spiritually.

Throughout my ministry, both as a parish pastor and teacher, I have seen the prophets do the same things for many other people who have allowed them to become part of their existence. People loaded down with loneliness, despair, senses of purposelessness, and many of the other problems that beset all of us at one juncture of our existence or another have had the lives and words of these Old Testament

saints become sources of strength and hope. I am convinced
that they can serve as sources for understanding and renewal
for others of this generation and ones yet unborn, including
you!

In the preparation of this book I have had the assistance of
a number of people. Albert P. Stauderman, editor of *The
Lutheran*, graciously gave permission to reproduce in this
work much of the material that appeared in that periodical.
For his generosity I am deeply grateful.

I also am indebted to Betty Webb, my superb secretary,
for her preparation of the original manuscript. Typing and
retyping these chapters as they developed was a chore she
performed with amazing speed and great accuracy, along with
cheerfulness and a sense of humor.

Most of all I thank my wife, Rosemarie, and my four
children, Frank, Dora, Darrell, and Kimberly, for bearing
with me through the months spent in research, reflection,
and writing that gave this book birth. At last we are able to
do together once more those many things that make all our
lives richer and warmly intertwined.

1 PROPHECY—
"THE WORD OF THE LORD CAME . . ."

A few years ago, while I was visiting Boston, I happened to wander into a store that displayed a wonderful collection of posters. My eye happened to notice hanging above the entrance one poster which the artist had entitled "The Making of a Prophet." It was a humorous scene depicting a scrawny lad almost knocked flat by what was happening to him. With his knees sagging, his mouth agape, and his eyes nearly bulging out of his head, he was gazing up at a cloud suspended overhead out of which lightning was flashing.

In the center of the cloud one could make out an eye, and a voice was radiating from the mist. Transfixing the newly-made prophet, the voice boomed out, "Well then, my son, having said 'Yes,' how would you like to have your goose cooked now?"

While that poster and its quip do not present a verbatim account of any *specific* making of a prophet, at least as the Bible records it, the cartoon does depict some of the aspects that surround the summoning of those persons. The prophetic call did come from God, the message delivered was, indeed, the Lord's, and the position did involve goose-cooking on more than one occasion. And, to boot, the people to whom the call went out from God were more often than not the most surprised persons around that of all folks available for such a commission God should have fingered them out for so arduous and awesome a task.

Each of these aspects needs to be kept in mind as we prepare to listen to the messages of seven great prophets who lived and labored nearly twenty-eight hundred years ago. The specific backgrounds for each of the Hebrew prophets will be dealt with in detail when we look at the emphases of their individual books. However, before we treat them individually it is important to take an overall look at the basic characteristics of the Old Testament prophets as a group. Individuals all, each with particular traits unique to himself, there were a number of similarities which they all shared and which set them apart as peculiar spokesmen for God.

If there is one characteristic that was common to all biblical prophets it was their absolute assurance that God had called them personally into his service. The Hebrew term which we translate into English as "prophet" is *nabi*. In its root sense it means "the one who was called." In every instance that call was understood by the persons who received it to have been a divine one. When it came to the making of a prophet, no human selection committee was involved in the appointment of any of these spokesmen of the Lord.

As even a quick reading of their books reveals, the specific calls came to the various prophets in a variety of ways. Jeremiah, for instance, understood himself to have been ordained by God before his conception to be "a prophet to the nations" (Jer. 1:5). Amos, on the other hand, was a herdsman and a tender of "sycamore trees," whom God ordered to "go, prophesy" when an adult (Amos 7:14-15). The great Isaiah was serving as a priest when he heard God's call for a messenger during a temple service (Isa. 6:1-8). Hosea, a family man, received his call through his personal crisis and marital difficulties (Hos. 1:1-11).

Despite all of this diversity, each person understood his selection somehow to have been a divine one. The only self-made or self-determined prophets in biblical history were those who proved to be false ones. The mark of each true prophet was that he or she had a personal experience with God, though not always knee-buckling in character, that proved that God, and not someone else, had chosen him or her for the task. Hence, in a very special sense, right from the beginning the prophets understood themselves to be God's handpicked spokesmen and his personal messengers.

The prophetic utterances, likewise, were understood by them to be God's words, not the prophet's own concoctions. Although the voice did not always come to the prophets out of a cloud, their words were not sermons which the prophets composed and then delivered to their contemporaries in God's behalf. Time and again the prophetic speeches are introduced with such telling statements as "This is the message which the Lord gave Hosea . . ." (Hos. 1:1), "God revealed these things to (Amos) about Israel . . ." (Amos 1:1), "This is the message which the Lord gave to Micah . . ." (Mic. 1:1) to verify that *God*, not the prophet, was the author of what was about to be said.

Only when such divine messages were received did the true prophet speak, act, or write. In fact, there were periods of silence for all of the prophets, as the short length of most of their books attests. As Jeremiah reports, he had to wait ten days on one occasion before the Lord gave him the answer to an issue he had posed and to which he wanted a response to deliver (Jer. 42:1ff.). Indeed, one of the signs of a self-appointed, and therefore false, prophet was that he or she acted and spoke without God's appointment and prompting (Jer. 14:14-15). Such antics resulted in such people giving "a lying vision, worthless divination, and the deceit of their own minds" (Jer. 14:14).

The third characteristic of prophetic messages and the prophets themselves was that both were radically conservative ethically, socially, and theologically. Contrary to many recent opinions, the prophets were not persons who broke with their religious traditions and then challenged others to bury their heritage with them. The fact is that the prophets were staunch advocates of the religious heritage from which they sprang, and continually called upon their contemporaries to embrace and live out the values they had been taught by God long before, values which they personally had promised to incorporate into their own life-styles. It is true that the prophets were *radicals* in the core sense of the word. They drove to the root of the issues that confronted them in their ministry, which is what the term "radical" means. They were driven to deal with the heart of the problems that beset society, not just play with the peripheral things that surround them.

Moreover, they did so as members of the believing community, calling to errant brothers and sisters who were in the same faith tradition as they to reform and live out their lives in line with the word of God given through the ages. It is a mistake, therefore, to depict the prophets as wild-eyed loners standing outside of the fellowship of Israel addressing an "alien" group, hopelessly trapped by outdated "traditions." If anything, the prophets saw themselves as *belonging* to the people to whom they were called to minister. This is an extremely important point to keep in mind in an age when we are being bombarded by individuals who would tell us that being prophetic means setting oneself against, and apart from, the organized church or traditional faith community. They would have us believe that even to identify oneself as a member of that faith community is repugnant to the Lord! Such an attitude was foreign to the prophets we will be studying. While thundering for change within society and individual lives, they pressed God's case for both as members of the religious community they were challenging. For it was that believing community, which for all of its warts, distortion, and failures in the past, in fact produced the very ones God called to be his prophetic messengers! It was through Israel that God sorted when he was making his selection of the appropriate people to be his spokesmen.

The prophets did not drop from heaven on parachutes or hatch in strange lands under rocks. They arose from the people of God, where they most often had been bred, nurtured, trained, and at times even supported in their work. As they carried out their mission they drew upon the religious heritage which they held in common with the people to whom God had sent them, as Micah himself pointed out when he stood and preached to the people of Israel, "[The Lord] *has told* us what is good. What he requires of us is this, to do what is just, show constant love, and humbly obey our God" (Mic. 6:8, italics added). Micah, as would be true of his prophetic colleagues that followed him, rarely delivered new or novel messages to his hearers. The word that God moved him and them to speak was a word which most of the people had heard many times before. What the prophets were called to do was, as one Israelite to other Israelites, move their people to be faithful to a heritage they together professed and which they had sworn to obey in dealing with God and each other. The prophetic challenges for the future continually were made on an appeal to their common traditions which God was pressing them all to enflesh anew. That call for personal renewal was radical in its efforts to conserve what was best for society based upon their experience with God.

A fourth characteristic of the prophets was that they generally were laypersons. Except for Moses, Isaiah, Jeremiah, and Ezekiel, all of the other prophets, as far as we know, were laypeople. Whether these spokesmen of the Lord continued to function in their normal trades alongside of their prophetic ministries is not usually revealed in their books. Judging from the few sermons or acts contained in the writings attributed to them, it appears probable that either their prophetic occasions came as scattered periods in their day-to-day functions or that their prophetic careers were short-lived, being confined to a few years, or even weeks, during which they left their homes and trades to speak and act for the Lord.

Apparently not many of the prophets had happy lives, in a generally accepted sense of that term. Hosea's home was torn by the adultery of his wife. Amos faced opposition from the priest Amaziah, who went to the king with his charges of sedition against the prophet (Amos 7:10ff.). Jeremiah was ostracized by his contemporaries, forcing him to cry out in his loneliness (Jer. 12:7-11). He later was publicly humiliated and branded as a traitor, being thrust into prison for his efforts at saving the nation. One of Jeremiah's contemporaries, a prophet named Uriah, faired even worse. He was put to death by King Jehoiakim, who murdered him with the royal sword for preaching essentially the same message in

Jerusalem which Jeremiah himself proclaimed (Jer. 26:20).
Jesus later was to sum up this lot of the prophets when he
looked over Jerusalem during his processional entry into that
city and wept:

> O Jerusalem, Jerusalem, *killing the prophets* and *stoning those
> who are sent to you!* How often would I have gathered your
> children together as a hen gathers her brood under her wings, and
> you would not! (Luke 13:34, italics added)

The lives of most of the prophets probably were difficult
because the messages God delivered through them placed
them frequently in opposition roles in relationship to their
contemporaries. Being sent by God to challenge corruption
among the common as well as the mighty people meant for
most of them being met with hostility and rage on the part of
the persons whose sins they fingered. Despite such attitudes,
one of the distinguishing traits of the vast majority of biblical
prophets was that they continued to love the people they
addressed regardless of their response to them. This held true
even for those difficult situations when their preaching fell
on apparently stopped-up ears.

With Hosea as one of their outstanding examples, the
prophets tended to be forgiving and hopeful individuals
despite the fact that they had few apparent reasons for being
so when they looked for some signs of potential change in
the lives of the people they engaged. Their messages, as we
shall see, are shot through with the optimistic call for people
to remake their lives. If that call is to be taken seriously, then
we must assume that the prophets believed that the people to
whom they preached could in fact alter their conduct. If that
were true, then the chance for changing the course of an
individual life, a community, or a nation always existed, no
matter how depressing the future appeared to be. The
prophets clung doggedly to this conviction that even a badly
corrupted social order had the potential of being turned
around with God's help and the willingness of the people to
take advantage of that chance for a new day which the Lord
continually was providing for them. This is one of the main
reasons that even the most gloomy of the prophets, such as

some claim Amos to be, has rays of hope for a better tomorrow shining through his most dour warnings of potential catastrophe. Even the harsher predictions of doom are usually couched in settings of possible restoration. And it is this combination of confrontation and compassion which, I feel, has kept the prophets in the forefront of our religious heritage.

Because these spokesmen for God all saw life without misty-eyed illusions, their value has not faded through the thousands of years that separate them from us. The situations they addressed remain with us still, simply being updated in dress and dropped in contemporary settings. This being so, the prophets are not just figures *from* and *for* the past. But they, and their more contemporary successors, still are able to walk up and tap us in our consciences, probing us to get our lives in order individually and with one another.

2 MOSES: COVENANT

In his *Frieze of the Prophets,* painted on the wall of the Boston Public Library, John Singer Sargent's long line of God's greatest "forth-tellers" is dominated by the magnificent figure of Moses. Standing between Elijah and Joshua, Moses looms large with his hands holding upright the two great tablets of the Ten Commandments. He is the one to whom all eyes are drawn as though they were being pulled by magnets.

In making Moses the focal point in that train of mighty people, Sargent has given us an accurate assessment of Moses' place in Israelite history. He does bestride the Old Testament like a colossus, embodying in himself at one time or another nearly every function or office important to the life and development of his people. He is slave and nobleman, man-killer and judge, reluctant leader and absolute ruler, as well as shepherd, prophet, and priest! In a measure never again matched, even by one so mighty as King David, Moses almost single-handedly shaped the character of the Hebrews. Indeed, perhaps as an acknowledgment of his uniqueness, not another man in the biblical narrative ever again was to bear his name in the procession of biblical heroes.

The basic information about this giant of our heritage is carried in many places in the Bible, although no record of Moses exists in any other known literature of the period. A good Bible concordance will help locate the specific references to Moses in both the Old and New Testaments. Most of them cluster in the books of Exodus, Leviticus, Numbers, Deuteronomy, and Joshua, with the books of Kings (1 Kings 2–8; 2 Kings 14–23) and Chronicles (1 Chron. 6–26; 2

Chron. 1–8; 23–35) giving us added details about his life and activities. What emerges from a study of these references is the portrait of a man almost superhuman in some aspects, while at other times as earthy and approachable as a friendly personal acquaintance.

The basic story line of Moses' life is so full that even Cecil B. De Mille was not able to encompass it! Intertwined with the miraculous and romantic incidents of his life are many hard and gutty moments. Even the most sketchy outline of his "career" points up the awesome ups and downs in Moses' lifetime, any peak or valley of which would probably be able to encompass the totality of your life or mine.

Moses was born into an apparently hopeless situation probably early in the thirteenth century B.C. when the Hebrews were slaves held in bondage by the Egyptians. At that particular time in history, the Egyptians were planning the decimation of their Hebrew slaves. Fearing that the Israelite population could be the backbone for a future attempt to subvert and take over their realm, the Egyptians attempted to thin their numbers by killing all male babies born to the Israelites (Exod. 1:15-16). When Moses was born his mother hid him for three months (Exod. 2:1-2). Fearing his discovery, she put him into a bassinet made seaworthy with pitch and set him afloat in the midst of some reeds by the riverbank, where by chance a childless daughter of Pharaoh discovered him, fished him from the waters, and adopted him as her own son. The name the princess gave him is the one by which we all subsequently have come to know him. "Moses" is an Egyptian name derived from a root which means "to draw out" or "draw up." What his Hebrew name may have been, if in fact he had been given one, has been lost. Even though he was returned to his mother for wet-nursing (Exod. 2:7-10), he was eventually taken as a child into the Egyptian court of Pharaoh to be raised and trained as a prince of the realm.

What is often overlooked by many people is the fact that until he became an adult Moses was essentially a member of the Egyptian nobility. Like the other princes of the land produced by the many sons and daughters of the Pharaoh, he would have received the necessary training in warfare, finance, religion, and diplomacy to qualify him for service to the state, and possibly for the role of Pharaoh itself. Not only did Moses in these early years learn the customs of the people he was to set himself against, but he became an integral part of the family from which came the ruler of the nation he later was to face when he fought for the freedom of the Hebrews. The Pharaoh he was to challenge was a relative through adoption and a man whom he no doubt had known personally.

The act of killing an Egyptian taskmaster whom he saw abusing a Hebrew slave (Exod. 2:11-15) eventually led to Moses' fleeing the realm to save himself from punishment. Going into the desert of Midian, an area located in the Sinai peninsula, he met the family of a priest named Jethro, whose daughter Zipporah he later married. Taking up the life of a shepherd, he roamed the rocky, barren area through which years later he was to lead the Hebrews in their journey to freedom.

It was while wandering through the mountains of the area that Moses investigated a bush on fire upon the hillside, and in the effort met God in a life-changing encounter (Exod. 3:1ff.). Through the bush Yahweh called Moses to go back to Egypt to lead the Hebrew slaves from bondage. He was directed to go to Pharaoh and call for his people's release, and to demonstrate through a series of wondrous acts the fact that his demands were backed by the Lord. Though with great reluctance and often repeated efforts to have God choose someone else for the position, Moses retraced his steps to the royal court. What followed is one of the greatest epics in the battle for human freedom in recorded history.

When Moses pled with the Pharaoh, probably the great Ramses II (1290-1224 B.C.), to free the Hebrews, he was met with rebuff. To pressure the Egyptians to release his people, a series of plagues was sent on the oppressors in an ascending order of severity (Exod. 7:1ff.). The Hebrew word for these plagues, *nagah,* means essentially "to strike," "to hit." Each stroke God levied was intended to open the hand of the slaveholder and force the release of his captives. Not until the mighty blow of a plague that cost the lives of the Egyptians' children, however, did the Pharaoh issue the order for freedom.

But that freedom appeared to be short-lived. Hardly had the people moved out before Pharaoh and his army were in hot pursuit of them. Catching the Hebrews at the banks of the "Yam Suf," or "Sea of Reeds" (identified in some Bible translations as the Red Sea), the precise location of which has not been established for certain, the first miracle of the journey occurred (Exod. 14:1ff.). As Moses "stretched out his hand over the sea" (Exod. 14:21), the waters parted to allow the former slaves to pass and then rolled back to drown the pursuing Egyptian army which rushed into its midst to attempt to recapture the fleeing Israelites. With Moses as the "worker," a series of miracle-signs of God's presence and power followed the people on their movement toward the land of Canaan, which God had promised as their future home. Water emerged from rock (Exod. 17:1ff.), food appeared before the hungry people, and divine guidance was provided both day and night. This sustenance enabled Moses to lead the company on toward the mountain that was to be the first destination of the journey.

At Mount Sinai, a peak whose location is not certain, God made a covenant with the Hebrews using Moses as his go-between in the process (Exod. 19ff.). Since they had been freed from servitude, the compact in which the Lord bound *himself* to the *people*, they bound *themselves* to *Him*, and all bound *themselves* to *one another* outlined the principles for living which were designed by God to enable his people to throw off forever the shackles of tyranny and servitude. The provisions of the covenant were intended to keep all the people from using their freedom to make themselves and each other slaves once more to life-styles that would lead eventually to other kinds of bondage. That event marked the moment at which the people of Israel began their great advance into nationhood. On the sacred mountain in the wilderness the pact of holiness and love was *experienced*, and from that point on it was to become the pattern for their lives as individuals and as a society.

For the Hebrews, the covenant was *good news*, that is "gospel" not "law." In it God pledged himself to be loyal to his nation as the people in turn pledged their ultimate commitment to him and the fundamental values he embodied in his relationship to them and the world. This mutual *binding* together of the Israelites with their Lord, which is what the Hebrew term for covenant, *berith*, really means, was in many ways like a marriage ceremony. The two covenantal partners so loved each other that they pledged to live in faithfulness together with no termination clause included!

This basis of love rather than force for the covenant is made abundantly clear in the Hebrew text that describes the event and the provisions of the pact that were to characterize the values and principles by which the Israelites were to shape their existence. The core of these pointers for life, which we call "commandments," in Hebrew are simply referred to as the "words" which the Lord spoke to the people through Moses (Exod. 20:1). What may be surprising to some people is that these ten "words" were not thundered out by God as orders, but were delineated by him as prescriptions for true peace and harmony for the ones to whom they were directed.

Most of the commandments as they exist in our Hebrew texts are written in the grammatical form known as the indicative rather than the imperative. Only two of the ten, the ones referring to keeping the Sabbath and the honoring of parents, are given in Hebrew as commands and ought to be translated into English as direct orders. The other eight "words," to be properly translated, should read "You *will* not," not "You *shall* not." Not only does such a rendering transmit the Hebrew text in its proper sense, but it helps us to get hold of the undergirding spirit of these guides for life by the right end.

The covenant which the Lord made with the Hebrews in the wilderness was not a completely new one. Long before the time of Moses the Lord had singled out the great patriarch of the Old Testament, Abraham, and entered into a similar bond with him. A persistent lover, God had searched the earth for someone sensitive enough to understand his longings for fellowship and respond positively to them. When he found such a man in Abraham the basis for the relationship that he was to forge with his servant was set out in a concise and far-reaching formula: "You will be my people and I will be your God" (Exod. 6:7).

The generations that succeeded Abraham saw themselves as being heirs to the covenant God had made with their forefather. Certainly at least some of those who went down into Egypt in the time of Jacob to buy grain, and remained there ultimately to become the slaves who built the storehouse cities for Ramses the Great, remembered the pact made in ages past in which God had promised to remember them and preserve them from extinction. Hence, when Moses led the people to the mountain in the wilderness to again covenant with the gracious God who had thrown off the yoke of servitude they bore so bitterly, they already had experienced *personally* the mercy of the Lord they met at the "smoking mountain" (Exod. 20:18).

In the covenant forged at Sinai, Yahweh pledged to do for the nation all that a God could provide. He would watch over his people, supply their needs, and demonstrate his perpetual concern for the direction of their lives. His human covenanting partners, on the other hand, pledged themselves to respond to him in a way that demonstrated the love they felt for their God. They would live out that love for him, respect him, serve him, and obey him. In a nutshell, they committed themselves to be as faithful to him as he had been, and would be, to them. Hence, the way they would order their lives in living with God and one another would be determined principally by how much each one meant to the other. That is, they would respond to one another because of *love* for the covenant partner to whom they had been linked.

The book of Deuteronomy, in which the covenant event at Sinai is central, is one in which the term we translate into

English as "love," the Hebrew *ahev*, is predominant. In fact, "love" appears in that writing more often there than in any books of the New Testament with the exception of the Gospel and Epistles of John! The term *ahev* in its root sense means "to demonstrate affection," "to show great esteem and commitment." As with other Hebrew verbs and nouns, the reality of the "sentiment" or "attitude" was assumed to be testable by actions and activities that could be seen and experienced in the realm of human relationships. The Hebrew mind-set was one which held to the premise that an individual *does* love, not just *"feels"* it. A person lives lovingly in his or her interactions with another, and does not just voice warm sentiments. For to the Israelites love always was expected to find concrete, tangible expression if it was truly present and alive. If such expressions did not emerge in the life-styles of professed "lovers," then serious doubts arose about the genuineness of one's claims.

Because they loved God more than anything else in life, the covenant assumed that the people of Israel would live in ways that demonstrated their love for God. Since the Lord was the key person for them, then it would follow as a matter of course that they would have "no other gods before [him]" (Exod. 20:1-6), that they would treat his name with reverence (Exod. 20:7), and that they would provide time in which they would step apart from day-to-day affairs to remember God's creative work in fashioning the world (Exod. 20:8-11).

In addition, they would relate to everyone and everything he created in ways modeled by God's own dealings with both. If God were indeed the father of all people, then they were to live in relationship with one another in ways that demonstrated that they knew they were brothers and sisters. Hence, they would honor their parents (Exod. 20:12), they would not murder each other (Exod. 20:13), or lie about and slander each other (Exod. 20:16), or defraud, covet, and steal from one another (Exod. 20:16, 17), or degrade one another (Exod. 20:14). Though *other* people who did not acknowledge God as the pacesetter for their lives might do such things, they would not, because of his love for them and their love for him. They would willingly attempt to shape their lives in ways that would be pleasing to him and good for each other.

The covenant and its provisions were not made or given for the good of God but for the good of the people themselves. If they refused to shape their lives according to its provisions, that in no way affected God's position as Lord. He was God whether they acknowledged it and lived their lives in light of it or not! Should they be so foolish as to ignore God's leading toward full freedom and escape from bondage of one sort or another, then the ones who would, and do, suffer for their foolishness would be themselves and society.

In an effort to prevent such a squandering of life, God lovingly had set before his people the way to peace and true fulfillment in the covenant. If you look at the covenant provisions you will note that the ten "words," or commandments, are based upon a high view of the worth of people. The base on which they all rest is the conviction that human beings are the highest forms of God's creative activity. The commandments assume the basic equality of all people. The covenant "words" make specific what the creation story in Genesis 1:26-31 points out in a more narrative way, that all people, races, and sexes come from a single creative act of the Lord and all have equal value and dignity. There are no double standards written into the "words" so that one person is set above or below another. Each human being, king or beggar, clergy or layperson, has value. Each of us has worth not because of what we are able to do or possess, or the "connections" we may have established, but because we are human beings. Whether women or men, white or people of color, mentally retarded or geniuses, multitalented or one-talented, each ought to be treated and regarded as holy people created by God. Each human being, by virtue of his or her personhood, is to be related to lovingly!

Moreover, the covenant assumes that all of us were made to live in relationship to other human beings. You and I were created by God for communal living, not for existence in isolation from others. Though it may be possible for animals who are raised in isolation to mature as reasonable types of their breed, where human beings are concerned reaching full personhood demands that we relate to others of our "species" and in the interaction learn from, and with, each other the basic lessons of what it means to be human.

The resulting interaction demands that we accept and order our existence by certain principles and priorities so that we do not destroy one another. Such restraints can be accepted as necessary parts of life so that each has space to develop as an individual, while allowing others to do the same. The violation of other human beings, and their rights, cannot be endured or tolerated for long without disaster being the consequence for all society. In order that integrity and freedom be available to all, styles of life must be developed that are lived within guidelines that direct us toward heightened appreciation for the worth of all elements in God's creation. This is one of the other bases on which the biblical understanding of covenant and its guiding principles is built.

The assumption that is implicit in both making and living out the covenant is that people should strive to order their lives according to the covenant's prescriptions. Even Jesus expected that the life-style called for by the ten "words" should be lived out by the people he met (see Mark 10:17-22; Luke 10:25-28). God had built into each human being at her/his creation the potential to live according to his will. With his continued help, pull, direction, and encouragement, he expected those who bound themselves to him to reflect in their relations with him and each other the principles they pledged themselves to observe when the covenant was affirmed.

That they had this potential to do so did not mean that the people Moses led were to have an easy time in shaping their lives according to the covenant's prescriptions. Time and again they were to fail, individually and collectively. But despite the failures, which he personally experienced both in himself and in others, Moses continued to challenge his people to turn their lives in more positive directions. His challenge was that those who called Yahweh "Lord" should lovingly serve Him with faithfulness and dedication, and deal humanely with the other human beings whose lives they affected in the day-to-day realm of experience.

From Mount Sinai, Moses led the developing nation for more than forty years in a journey through the wilderness of Sinai and southern Palestine (Num. 10:11ff.). In these four decades the struggle of learning to live in harmony with each other, battles for self-preservation among hostile nations, and the preparation and training for nationhood as well as for taking possession of the "promised land" all challenged the limits of Moses' leadership resources. With no precedents to follow in nation-building, but relying on God's guidance and his own stamina and wits, he was gradually able to shape the often recalcitrant mob into a hardy "people." Under these most austere circumstances, Moses molded the basic character and faith of the nation for the next three thousand years.

Although Moses died just before the land of Canaan was entered, having been allowed to view it from east of the Jordan River, the people he trained eventually reached their destination under the leadership of Joshua. While the specific place of Moses' burial has never been located, his memorial lives on in the Hebrew-Christian tradition he helped initiate and sharpen. His faith in one God who was the Lord of all creation, his untiring efforts to train his people in faithfulness to their Lord and in the appreciation of their value as people created by God, and his demonstration of moving forward to the beckoning of God under the most awesome and trying circumstances makes him stand front and center as an example of commitment and integrity. Others who followed him in the pages of the Old Testament, people like Joshua, David, and the prophets, made magnificent contributions to the history and faith of their people. But none ever reached the stature of this man who rose from the status of slave to become father of the faith. The footprints he left for future generations to follow are ones that have led billions of people where hope, wholeness, and the love of God have abounded.

3 ISAIAH:
SIN AND RESTORATION

In his *Frieze of the Prophets*, John Singer Sargent painted Isaiah, face turned toward heaven, in the purple robes of royalty. Whether Isaiah was born to the nobility of the nation or not, as tradition and some passages from his book may indicate, the man and his message truly stand out in the literature of the Bible as *noble* in the true sense of that term. His book is one of the most eminent ones, filled with a dignity, beauty, and soaring faith in God which at the same time calls for a living-out of one's faith in concrete, person-to-person terms.

Scholars still debate whether the entire book bearing Isaiah's name was written by a single individual. Some argue that only chapters 1 through 39 came from the Isaiah mentioned in the introduction to the text (1:1ff.). They speculate that chapters 40 through 55 were written by someone living during the period of the Exile (587-539 B.C.) and that chapters 55 through 66 are the work of a third prophet who worked and wrote following the return of the nation to its home territory after 539 B.C. Regardless of how the question of authorship has been resolved, universally the judgment has remained that the entire book ranks as one of the outstanding portions of Holy Scriptures.

For about four decades the son of Amoz (not to be confused with Amos, a prophet who was an earlier contemporary of Isaiah), born probably around 760-755 B.C., labored in Judah, warning, challenging, and encouraging his people and kings to follow Yahweh's directions for their lives. He is the only spokesman for the Lord whom the Bible records as having married a prophetess (Isa. 8:3). The couple had two

sons, Maher-shalal-hash-baz (8:3) and Shear-jashub (7:3),
who apparently were born prior to Isaiah's beginning his prophetic ministry. According to his own testimony, Isaiah
received his prophetic summons in the year that King Uzziah
died (742 B.C.), when he was caught up in a vision during his
visit to the temple (6:1ff.). Responding to the divine call for
a messenger with, "Here am I! send me," he entered a time of
service to the Lord that spanned the reign of Jotham
(742-735 B.C.) and Ahaz (735-715 B.C.) and extended into
that of Hezekiah (715-687 B.C.)—all of whom were kings of
Judah.

From the beginning of his ministry Isaiah was an extra-
ordinary person. Unlike many of the other prophets, he
seemed to have ready access to all of the monarchs who were
on the throne during his adult lifetime, and apparently
related to them as peers. He frequently advised the rulers on
affairs of state (7:3-17; 8:1-6; 30:1-5; 31:1-3). He threatened
one of the highest royal officials (22:15ff.), apparently with
impunity. Indeed, his relations with Ahaz himself were signif-
icant enough that the king knew one of Isaiah's sons by name
(7:3)!

Because of this close relationship with the court, it is
sometimes conjectured that Isaiah himself was a member of
the royal family or class. No direct evidence exists to
substantiate such a claim. In fact, no clear definition of his
nonprophetic profession is possible from the data we have
available to us. Among the possibilities are that he may have
been a physician (38:21), a court annalist (1 Chron. 26:22),
or a priest/temple official, a position that would explain his
gaining close proximity to the Holy of Holies, the sacred
precinct of the temple where the Ark of the Covenant was
kept, an area in which he apparently was standing when he
had his vision of call (Isa. 6:1ff.).

In any case, Isaiah's functioning as God's spokesman took
him into the most prestigious places of the realm, the palace
and the temple, as well as into the city's streets and markets.
This broad experience helped give him the chance to view
and speak to all levels and aspects of life. Though the

specifics of his oracles and proclamations varied, the basic thrust of his message centered upon the call of God for the people of Judah to reverse their sinful life patterns. As he examined the contemporary scene it was evident to the prophet that the poor were being oppressed, justice was being perverted by an unjust legal system, the self-indulgence of the rich was rampant, the insatiable drive for power and wealth was evident everywhere, sham-full religious ceremonial was being carried on side-by-side with idolatrous practice and superstition, and political wheeling and dealing on the national and international level was being counted on to save the nation. Aware of the reality and righteousness of God, who desired above all else right behavior toward himself and one's fellow human beings, Isaiah pointed his people toward the fearful judgment that would fall on them all should they refuse to mend their ways. In a pronouncement that catches up the heart of his entire ministry he called the nation to

> Hear the word of the Lord
>   you rulers of Sodom!
> Give ear to the teaching of our God,
>   you people of Gomorrah!
> "What to me is the multitude of your sacrifices?
>   says the Lord;
> I have had enough of burnt offerings of rams
>   and the fat of fed beasts;
> I do not delight in the blood of bulls,
>   or of lambs, or of he-goats. . . .
>
>   (1:10-11)
>
> Wash yourselves; make yourselves clean,
>   remove the evil of your doings
>   from before my eyes;
> cease to do evil,
>   learn to do good;
> seek justice,
>   correct oppression;
> defend the fatherless,
>   plead for the widow."
>
>   (1:16-17)

Failure to shape their commitments, values, and lives along such lines would mean disaster for the people of Judah (1:20).

During the first period of his ministry (742-735 B.C.),

Isaiah time and again proclaimed the approach of the Day of the Lord. It was to be a time of national catastrophe. Because the nation had "forsaken the Lord . . . despised the Holy One of Israel . . . [and was] utterly estranged" (1:4), the sinful nation was headed for divine punishment (3:18-26).

The second period (735-715 B.C.) seems to have been one of silence for Isaiah. Declaring that he was going to "bind up the testimony, seal the teaching among my disciples [and] wait for the Lord, who is hiding his face from the house of Jacob" (8:16-17), he apparently kept his word and rarely addressed the nation during this period of Assyrian domination of his people.

In the third period (715-701 B.C.), which began with the death of Ahaz, Isaiah's public ministry reached full sway, being a time when he was able to establish intimate ties and relationships with Hezekiah, the king who succeeded Ahaz. Convinced that Assyria was God's agent in carrying out his judgment and punishment of sinful nations (10:5-10), Isaiah continually counseled Hezekiah to stay out of the revolts and plots against that superpower that periodically took shape among the nations Assyria had conquered and put under subjugation. When the Assyrian king Sargon died in 705 B.C., some of the conquered lands, including Babylon, and its ruler Merodach-baladan (ch. 39), used the occasion as a chance to declare their independence from their overlords. Isaiah advised the rulers of his nation against having Judah participate in the revolt. When the Ethiopians sent envoys to enlist Hezekiah as a partner in their alliance, Isaiah warned of the ultimate disaster that was to befall those who joined it (18:1-6).

In a series of powerful utterances Isaiah thundered that reliance on Egypt, the archrival of Assyria, to be the savior of his people was futile for Judah. Only reliance on God ultimately could prevent disaster from overtaking the land (chs. 28-31). When the king and populace turned a deaf ear to his warnings (22:1-14; 29:7-22) the Assyrian armies in about 701 B.C. overran Judah, ravaging many of her towns (2 Kings 18:13-37) under the leadership of King Sennacherib.

Sennacherib later had his campaign described on a clay cylinder which has since been discovered by archeologists. The description notes that he completed his march through Palestine by shutting up Hezekiah "like a caged bird in Jerusalem, his royal city."

Isaiah saw the seige of Jerusalem by the Assyrian king as God's punishment of Judah for its sins and moral and social corruption. But when Sennacherib's envoys reviled the "Holy One of Israel" (Isa. 37:8-13), Isaiah responded that Sennacherib would never take the city by conquest. "By the way that he came, by the same he shall return, and he shall not come into this city, says the Lord. For I will defend this city to save it, for my own sake and for the sake of my servant David." (Isa. 37:34-35; 2 Kings 19:34) Isaiah's prophecy was, in fact, fulfilled. Before Sennacherib could subjugate Jerusalem he was forced to return home to deal with a political upheaval in his own capital. His retreat, however, came only after Judah had suffered frightful losses to the Assyrian invaders.

The fourth period of his ministry (701-?) was one in which Isaiah seems to have gone into semi-retirement. Oracles such as those contained in Isaiah 2:1-5; 9:1-7; 11:1-9; 32:1-8, 15-18, 20 may come from this period when the prophet looked toward a time of universal peace and righteousness. The "messiah," mentioned in the latter passages, would usher in such an age which had eluded the kings and rulers who in Isaiah's lifetime banked more on shrewd political alliances than on the promises and strength of God to save their world. Scholars still debate over whether these prophesies of a Messiah relate primarily to the emergence of an earthly king or point toward a divine messenger who would miraculously make the dream a reality.

Isaiah himself did not live to see all nations say, "Come, let us go up to the mountain of the Lord, to the house of the God of Jacob; that he may teach us his ways and that we may walk in his paths" (2:3), or when the nations "beat their swords into plowshares, and their spears into pruning hooks" (2:4). Nevertheless, he remained convinced that a "remnant"

of his nation would survive the coming punishment to witness it (10:20-23; 11:11, 16). His faith in a God great and
forgiving enough to want that to happen, and powerful
enough to assure that it would occur, kept him not only
faithful but confident in his ministry until its end. This
legacy of faith is a gift he added to that of his book itself for
future generations, including you and me.

Isaiah has been rightly called the prophet of holiness. His
experience with God led him to sense the awesome purity
and righteousness of the Lord as well as the overwhelming
gap that existed between Him and the corruption he saw
among his human contemporaries as they dealt with one
another in day-to-day affairs. The issue was clearly stated by
Isaiah the day he experienced his "call" in the temple. There
in the midst of his encounter with the Lord he cried out:

> Woe is me! For I am lost; for I am a man of unclean lips, and I
> dwell in the midst of a people of unclean lips; for my eyes have
> seen the King, the Lord of Hosts! (6:5)

Red often looks more vivid when contrasted with white.
As Isaiah watched and lived with the people of his day, and
compared their life-styles with that called for by God, the
depth and breadth of their corrupt relationships with God
and their compatriots became so apparent that he was moved
to speak and act against the perversions he witnessed time
and time again! For Isaiah, as with the other spokesmen of
God who preceded and followed him, sin became a recurrent
issue with which he struggled and which he forcefully
assailed.

The specific charges Isaiah made against the nation were
numerous and varied. Many of them concerned violations of
the commandments which were linked to the covenant made
by God with his people at Sinai (see Exod. 20:1-17). Lying
(Isa. 30:9; 59:13), murder (1:21), adultery (57:3), and
idolatry (2:8, 20; 10:11) abounded around him. The Israelites had promised to embrace that handful of divinely
delineated provisions for living that God had placed in the
hands of Moses on the holy mountain in the wilderness. But
they abandoned those guidelines which their loving deity had

shown them in their desert journey from Egyptian slavery to
freedom, spelling pain and decay for the entire nation and its
inhabitants who had settled in the land of promise. Fairness,
value, and respect for human dignity, and undivided loyalty
to the Lord himself, had been lost, and the trampling of the
covenant provisions was the result.

Isaiah, as well as the other prophets, saw such sins as
concrete acts perpetrated by individuals and groups. Sin had
its roots in the heart, in Hebrew the *Lev*. While that term
usually refers to that specific organ of the human body, for
the Semites the heart, or the "inward parts," was the control
center for human action. It was the heart, not the brain, as in
our culture, that received, filtered, and deciphered the messages that a human being perceived. Once "processed," the
heart "directed" the course of action that was to follow.
Therefore, the condition or attitude of the heart was crucial
for the shaping of all relationships. If it was corrupt, the
trend of the life it controlled would be adversely affected. As
Isaiah pointed out in the beginning of his book, the entire
nation and its populace was sick: "From the sole of the foot
even to the head, there is no soundness in it, but bruises and
sores and bleeding wounds" (1:6).

The specific terms he used to describe the sins of the
nation point out the character of the individual deeds.
Looking at four of the many terms employed can give us
some feel for the range of the crimes being committed. The
term *chatah*, used in such passages as 1:18, 31:7, and 38:17,
is a marksman's term which means "to miss the target." It is
found in passages such as Judges 20:16, where the text reads
"every one could sling a stone at a hair, and not miss
[*chatah*]." The word was used to point out the incidents in
which specific, known, and accepted standards for conduct
were violated by persons who fell short, or got out of line
with, the norms God had set for the lives of his people. The
positive factor in such sinning was that there was no indication that the sinner had denied there *were* styles of life which
the Lord expected them to live out. The challenge was to
revamp their ways according to those directions which they
knew God wanted them to follow.

A second term used by Isaiah to describe the corruption of his contemporaries was *avar*. Used in 10:28; 23:2; 28:15; 29:5; 33:8; and 34:10, it means essentially "to cross over the line, to stray, to trespass." It depicts a person drifting or walking away from another, be that "other" God or a human companion. It has in mind an individual going beyond a boundary line or prescribed limit which has been set for her or him. Such a drifting into forbidden territory may be done consciously or by carelessness. In any event, the end result can be the same, that is, people end up in dangerous and off-limits circumstances. Distance develops between persons in such situations which can lead to a loss of a sense of caring or value for those beyond the line. In some types of trespassing, people may even get into areas of living which are virtual mine fields where they can be destroyed.

A third word found in this book to describe sins is *ashak* (see 30:12; 33:15; 59:13). This Hebrew term is usually employed to describe situations in which wrong is done to persons who are weak or without defense. It means literally "to extort, to handle roughly." Often it is used to spotlight instances where the persons who have the upper hand bully, or run roughshod over, those unable to protect themselves. It often includes physical violence of one sort or another done to those who are down and out.

The fourth term that appears in the indictment by the prophet of his contemporaries is *pasha* (1:2, 28; 43:27; 46:8). It is the worst kind of sin of which a person, or group, can be guilty. It means "to revolt" or "to rebel" against the Lord. While each of the other terms used to describe the actions of the people contain in them some sense even by the offenders that there are standards for conduct which are valid and ought to be followed, *pasha* points to people who deny that there exist any such standards which they ought to obey in reference either to God or to other human beings. No one has the right to set limits for them! People guilty of *pasha* in fact declare that they are cutting the ties with the one against whom they are revolting. By their actions they are in effect denying that they any longer have need for the one to whom they once had committed themselves.

When Isaiah uses *pasha* to describe the acts of the people of Israel against the Lord, he does it with a sense of horror, for such an action indicates that the individuals want to supplant God with themselves. They had decided to assume absolute authority in setting their own priorities and standards for living apart from their Creator and Savior. Isaiah saw that such a stance toward the Lord would lead to ultimate disaster. He was early aware of the fact which we all have to learn when we assume such attitudes ourselves, the fact that any human being, including you or me, makes a very poor deity. Most of us have more than we can handle keeping our individual lives functioning smoothly from day to day. Trying to do that minus God, then attempting to run the whole world according to our dictates in addition to that, quickly turns life into a nightmare for us all. Chaos results, individually and collectively, tearing to shreds homes, neighborhoods, and eventually entire nations as well as the globe on which we all rest.

Caring person that he was, and voicing the warnings and hopes of the loving God who had called him to help save his people from their own self-destructive ways, Isaiah challenged his contemporaries to turn their morals and faith in a new direction:

> Come now, let us reason together,
>   says the Lord:
> though your sins are like scarlet,
>   they shall be as white as snow;
> though they are red like crimson,
>   they shall become like wool.
> If you are willing and obedient,
>   you shall eat the good of the land;
> But if you refuse and rebel,
>   you shall be devoured by the sword;
>   for the mouth of the Lord has spoken.
>   (1:18-20)

In the preaching of Isaiah, redemption is one of the powerful and consistent themes he strikes. It seems that he hardly finishes thundering the Lord's judgment on his contemporaries when in almost the next breath he begins to preach about the possibility for a new chance at remaking the future through the mercy and with the help of God! Though the prophet often is sent by God to put his finger on the sins of his people, threatening ominous consequences should they fail to turn their lives around, he also is used by the Lord almost as frequently to deliver messages of hope. Hence, in Isaiah the twin roles of God as judge and savior are constantly kept moving back and forth before his people as the prophet first thunders indictments for moral corruption, and then follows with assurances that reconciliation and reunion will take place sometime in the future.

Isaiah's prophecy of the Lord's "universal reign of peace" (2:1-5) holds up the Lord's redemptive activity in the midst of his calling his fellow Israelites to account for their sins. The hammer-blows of the announcement of Jerusalem's potential destruction (1:7-9, 21-31) must have been still ringing in their ears when Isaiah went back to the inhabitants of Jerusalem with the announcement that annihilation of the nation was not God's intention. The days would come when out of the ruins that were going to be made of the city, it would again arise and become for the Israelites and the other nations of the world a meeting place where God would await them all as they flowed in a stream toward him as well as toward one another.

In this prophecy Isaiah has three major points to make. The first is that the temple mount, that is, the area on the hilltop known as Mount Zion, which includes the main temple complex and its court area, would again have God in residence (2:2ff.). The presence of the Lord in his house at that day would be a sign that he and his people are living in harmony once more.

Second, the people of Israel and many other nations would freely come to learn God's will for them, and would trust him to be their savior in time of stress and trouble (2:2b-4a). One of the charges Isaiah had lodged against the people was that they had sought such strength and help from human sources in the past, forsaking Yahweh in their chase to form alliances to save themselves. In the restoration, the people of Israel would not only be willing to hear the Lord's teaching, but actively seek it out. Their number would be enlarged, since the nations whose aid they once sought would now with them search for the Lord of them all. It would be a uniting of many elements of the Lord's creation under the kingship of God.

The third point made is that as a result of this new attitude toward, and in alliance with God, wars would cease and the implements of battle would be refashioned into tools of peaceful occupation. In an exact reversal of the process recorded in Joel 3:10, Isaiah proclaims:

> And they shall beat their swords into plowshares,
>   and their spears into pruning hooks;
> nation shall not lift up sword against nation,
>   neither shall they learn war any more.
> O house of Jacob,
>   come, let us walk
>   in the light of the Lord.
>
>   (2:4b-5)

The Lord is proclaiming to Isaiah in this prophecy that following the painful calamity which the people's sins are bringing upon them, an era of true peace will be ushered in for all mankind. While the passage does not contain the word "peace" itself to describe the situation that will prevail at that time, the Hebrew root for that word, *shalom*, does catch up what Isaiah envisioned. The "days to come" would have the world and God's people living in a condition, or state of relationship, which the Lord had intended for them from the beginning of creation. This is what the word *shalom* actually tries to describe.

"Peace," as we often think of it, is too weak a rendering of *shalom*. Shalom itself comes from an older Semitic word, *salamu*, which means "for things to be complete, in perfect working order." Unfortunately, when we use the term "peace" we often are referring to what more accurately should be described as an armistice. The term "armistice" is employed to describe the suspension of hostilities, even though the situation between peoples or nations is anything but in perfect working order! Two armies can be arranged in battle lines a mile apart, planning future skirmishes should

they become convinced that if they moved first they could
win, and yet since no shots are flying at the moment, some of
us describe the situation as "peace." Or, members of a family
can live in the same house refusing to talk to one another,
unable to share with each other, perhaps even despising each
other, and yet since no overt arguments are underway and no
screaming and shouting echo through the halls, that sometimes gets the label of "peace."

Shalom, however, as noted above, never really fits such
situations. To apply this term, hostility must itself truly cease
and the persons involved relate to one another as caring
human beings. Each must see the other as a member of a
family that God has created, and acknowledging him as Lord,
be willing to try to live together as he intended them to do
since the time that he made them! Only then, with real love
and respect flowing between the parties, can a state of true
shalom ever be seen to prevail.

In this magnificent prophecy in the second chapter of his
book, Isaiah envisions such a day actually occurring. He
declares that beyond the suffering and pain which sin will
cause for his nation, the day will come (2:1) when with
God's help a new Garden of Eden, as it was prior to the
perversion of sin, will exist again. But Isaiah does not nail
down *when* that vision will be realized for either his contemporaries or for us. He does not promise his people that
hard days are not ahead. Just the opposite probably will be
true. Nevertheless, someday in the future God will bring his
people out of the trauma they are going to experience as part
of their punishment and give them a chance for a new future
beyond that grief. Thus, in the midst of a bleak situation
Isaiah was able to hold out hope even for a nation of people
who on the basis of their track record in no way deserved it.
Such a new day would be possible because the God who had
sent him to minister to the nation was a merciful and loving
deity!

4 HOSEA: FORGIVENESS

Even though Hosea stands as one of the best-known prophets in the Bible, there is little information about him personally, either in his own writings or in other Old Testament books. This is especially surprising when we see that the prophecies of Hosea themselves are so intimately related to his own personal experiences, especially those surrounding his marriage and home. And yet, apart from the fact that his father's name is Beeri and that he married an adulterous woman named Gomer who bore him three children, little else is revealed about the man.

From Hosea's own statement, his ministry spanned the reigns of five kings, all of whom were named in the opening lines of his prophecies. Four of them, Uzziah (783-742 B.C.), Jotham (742-735 B.C.), Ahaz (735-715 B.C.), and Hezekiah (715-687 B.C.), ruled in the southern kingdom, Judah, which had its capital in Jerusalem. The fifth, Jeroboam II (786-746 B.C.), reigned in Samaria, capital of the northern kingdom of Israel. If Hosea, indeed, remained active until the time that Hezekiah was crowned king, there is no indication of any prophecies coming from that period following the annihilation of the northern kingdom. It is hard to imagine that had he still been functioning Hosea would not have referred to the collapse of that realm when the Assyrian king Shalmaneser V conquered that city and subjugated the northern kingdom in 722-721 B.C., carrying many of its citizens off into exile and resettling it with his own forces. Yet, no oracles from his book seem to indicate that such a calamity had struck during his lifetime.

When Hosea's prophetic career began, the northern kingdom was intact. The Syrian wars which had raged during much of the ninth century B.C. had ended and a time of great national prosperity was under way. The palaces of Samaria were being decked with gold and ivory, trade was flourishing, and the economy boomed. To most of his contemporaries life in their nation seemed to be on the upswing and everything was as it should be.

Beneath the veneer of this prosperity, however, injustice and corruption were rampant. The moral and ethical values which the Israelites had accepted as the people of God had been largely abandoned with disastrous consequences for the poor and weak members of the land. Oppression, theft, prostitution, and murder (Hos. 4:2) had all become commonplace in a nation which was able to accept them with growing callousness. The ten "words," or commandments, which the Israelites had accepted on Mount Sinai (Exod. 20:1-17) to be the guidelines by which they would shape their lives together and with the Lord, had been bent so out of shape as to have been nearly shattered in the intervening years. At Mount Sinai during the Exodus, the people of Israel had made promises in a covenant event, much like a marriage ceremony, in which God and his people bound themselves into an eternal partnership. While the Lord had kept *his* promises to his human partner, *they* had thrown him over in their pursuit of their own ends. "Unfaithfulness" (1:2) akin to the prophet's wife Gomer's action in leaving Hosea, a husband who loved and longed for her, characterized Israel's abandonment of God in order to give themselves to one idol after the other as convenience served.

> What shall I do with you, O Ephraim?
>   What shall I do with you, O Judah?
> Your love is like a morning cloud,
>   like the dew that goes early away.
> Therefore I have hewn them by the prophets,
>   I have slain them by the words of my mouth,
>   and my judgment goes forth as the light.
> For I desire steadfast love and not sacrifice,
>   the knowledge of God, rather than burnt offerings.
>   (6:4-6)

This shattering of the covenant bond, and the social and personal crimes which followed, formed the arena in which the prophecies of Hosea were delivered. He was sent by God to recall the nation to faithfulness to their Lord and to each other. God was chasing Israel, as Hosea chased Gomer, in an attempt to rewin the people he loved after they had deserted him for others:

> Therefore, behold, I will allure her,
>   and bring her into the wilderness,
>   and speak tenderly to her.
> And there I will give her her vineyards,
>   and make the Valley of Achor a door of hope.
> And there she shall answer as in the days of her youth,
>   as at the time when she came out of the land of Egypt.
>
> And in that day, says the Lord, you will call me, "My husband," and no longer will you call me, "My Baal." For I will remove the names of the Baals from her mouth, and they shall be mentioned by name no more.   (2:14-17)

The book of Hosea is one long plea by God to a hardening and recalcitrant people to turn their lives and relationships around before total destruction would befall them individually and collectively.

Hosea had experienced Yahweh as a merciful God first-hand. He also came to learn during his lifetime that mercy, though it is always undeserved, is not a fact or term that is interchangeable with stupidity or softheadedness! Hosea knew that while God is loving and forgiving, he is one who at the same time calls for accountability for their actions on the part of the people toward whom his heart is continually opened:

> Like a stubborn heifer,
>   Israel is stubborn;
> can the Lord now feed them
>   like a lamb in a broad pasture?
> Ephraim is joined to idols,
>   let him alone.
> A band of drunkards, they give themselves to harlotry;
>   they love shame more than their glory.
> A wind has wrapped them in its wings,
>   and they shall be ashamed because of their altars.
> Hear this, O priests!
>   Give heed, O house of Israel!
> Hearken, O house of the king!
>   For the judgment pertains to you;

> for you have been a snare at Mizpah,
> and a net spread up on Tabor.
> (4:16—5:1b)

When immorality abounded (see chs. 4-10), Hosea predicted that punishment for it, in one form or another, was not only inevitable but already on its way (5:2). Through experience he also came to perceive that the purpose of such chastisement was God's attempt to bring sometimes hardheaded and corrupt people to their senses short of destruction. In fact, the Hebrew term often translated "punish" as it is used in Hosea 5:2 is *musar*. Its essential meaning is "to teach," or "to instruct." *Musar* describes God's attempt to help set people on the right track by reeducating and redirecting their attitudes and their lives. Indeed, one of the lessons Hosea teaches through his prophecies is that the Lord he worshiped is, in fact, such a loving teacher, not a hard-nosed, vindictive taskmaster.

Hosea sensitively portrayed this multifaceted dimension of God as both wooer and Lord throughout his book. His work is filled with the tender language and images of deep, warm, and caring family "feelings" which Yahweh continued to have for his people despite the trend of their lives (see 2:2ff.). As we shall see in the next two chapters dealing with Hosea and his prophecies, no matter how desperate the human predicament ever becomes, God continues to "hang in" in an effort to save from disaster those he created. This divine quality shines through in the final verses of the second chapter of the book where through the mouth of his spokesman God reassures his people:

> And I will betroth you to me for ever; I will betroth you to me in righteousness and in justice, in steadfast love, and in mercy. I will betroth you to me in faithfulness; and you shall know the Lord. . . .

> And I will have pity on Not pitied,
> and I will say to Not my people, "You are my people";
> and he shall say, "Thou art my God."
> (2:19-20, 23)

As already pointed out, God, as Hosea experienced him,

was a passionate, loving, and tender deity who often spoke with great warmth and feeling about the nation he called his own. Even after times when they deeply disappointed him by their vicious dealings with one another or with him, for which warnings of divine punishment were sent through the prophet, God often turned in an attempt to reembrace the wayward people of Israel. Even in the heat of anger, his love was never lost. A case in point is in chapters 11 and 12, where following the recitation of a long list of calamities that are in store for Israel should she not turn from her sins, Hosea records God's tender and moving hymn of love for the people he shaped with his own hands.

Recalling the days when he carried and led his people much like infants through the desert after rescuing them from Egypt, God opens his heart to the nation whose punishment he has already decreed. In a series of father-child vignettes, the Lord recalls how he gently tried to train the Israelites from their infancy to develop into mature and honorable men and women.

> When Israel was a child, I loved him;
>   and out of Egypt I called my son.
> The more I called them,
>   the more they went from me;
> they kept sacrificing to the Baals,
>   and burning incense to idols.
> Yet it was I who taught Ephraim to walk,
>   I took them up in my arms;
>   but they did not know that I healed them.
> I led them with cords of compassion,
>   with the bands of love,
> and I became to them as one
>   who eases the yoke on their jaws,
>   and I bent down to them and fed them.
>   (11:1-4)

Like a parent teaching a toddler to walk, he had taken them by the hand to support them in their first steps toward adulthood as they first struggled to gain their feet (11:3). And yet, for all of the intimacy and tenderness displayed (11:4), the response he got from the peoples he embraced was rejection. With the legs *he* had trained to walk with *him*, they ran in search of others to whom they could give themselves!

In such circumstances even divine love cannot forever hold off the consequences for the actions (11:7). Indeed, if the love of a parent for a child is great enough, sometimes sharp jolts may have to be administered to turn a child away from a trend of life that ultimately might kill him or her. At moments such as that the pain that is inflicted needs to be seen as love's response to desperate situations, as I learned in dealing with my own first son.

When my youngster reached the age when he began to walk, he delighted in making excursions over the floors of our home, constantly reaching out for the new attractions that he found scattered all around him. From toys, to slippers, to table tops, to desk drawers he crawled and rolled, feeling his way around the new world that had been opened to him. But in his travels one particular item caught his fancy. He developed a fascination for electric lamp cords, which he not only tried to tug out of their outlets but loved to jam into his mouth!

Needless to say, his mother and I became frantic over the latter. In an attempt to break that habit we first tried carrying him away from the cords that he touched. When that failed we upped the ante for his persistence by shaking a finger and giving stern commands when we caught him gnawing on the cords with his sharp new teeth. None of these tactics had any effect. In fact, matters seemed to get worse. It was only then, after all else failed, that the last card was finally played. As *his* hand latched onto the cord in the wall, *our* hands caught him by the top of the diapers, and with a firm thump he got whacked on the rump, bringing wails of fright from his mouth and tears running down his cheeks.

That moment was as traumatic for us as it was for him, I suspect. The last thing we wanted to do was hurt that little toddler we both loved so much. But for his good, not ours, and to keep him alive, we applied pain to prevent even more drastic consequences. We loved him too much to let him go on and electrocute himself without our acting to prevent it.

Though multiplied a millionfold, Hosea saw God dealing with Israel in much the same way when it was heading for suicide:

> They shall return to the land of Egypt,
>   and Assyria shall be their king,
>   because they have refused to return to me.
> The sword shall rage against their cities,
>   consume the bars of their gates,
>   and devour them in their fortresses.
> My people are bent on turning away from me;
>   so they are appointed to the yoke,
>   and none shall remove it.
>
>   (11:5-7)

The God who was threatening to deliver punishment to turn
them away from their sins was the same God who had ten-
derly attempted to teach them to stand on their own feet.
The suffering that came in response to their acts was God's
passionate attempt to keep Israel from ultimate self-annihila-
tion.

The twelfth chapter of the book of Hosea needs to be seen
in this light. When viewed from this perspective, it compli-
ments the opening verses of chapter 11. In the days of Hosea,
as well as in this day when you and I are living out our lives,
neither God, nor his prophets, *because of their love*, can
possibly brush off lightly the sins that tear us and society
apart. Both God and his spokespeople care for us too much
to allow that to happen. It usually is God's last-ditch effort
to turn us into more positive life-styles when suffering and
sharp raps from the divine hand are laid on us. What a wonderful thing it is to have a God whose feelings for us are so
intense that he "hangs in" with us even when our personal
and world histories get desperate rather than abandon us!
What an added gift it is for him to turn from those painful
moments to remind us that a whole new start may be
possible for us in spite of our past. For beyond the trauma of
having to face the consequences for our sins, the divine forgiveness, as we shall soon see, is God's way of opening up a
new day and the possibility for a rich future for us all. At the
same time that he must raise welts on us individually or
collectively, our Lord is proclaiming to us as well as to our
forefathers in Hosea's day:

> How can I give you up, O Ephraim!
> How can I hand you over, O Israel!

> How can I make you like Admah!
>   How can I treat you like Zeboiim!
> My heart recoils within me,
>   my compassion grows warm and tender.
> I will not execute my fierce anger,
>   I will not again destroy Ephraim;
>   for I am God and not man,
>   the Holy One in your midst,
>   and I will not come to destroy.
>   (11:8-9)

Hosea saw the punishment of his people as the prelude to their renewal. Like the other prophets, while he focused clearly on the sins of the nation and their consequences, that was not his only prophetic theme. The possibility for divine forgiveness, and a chance for a new beginning, were realities he proclaimed as well. In fact, the former were really preliminaries aimed at making the latter occur.

With Hosea particularly, the *forgiving* quality of God is always kept front and center. God, who calls for integrity and mercy from his people, himself demonstrates those same characteristics to them in his own activity. The God-given opportunities to cut themselves loose from their corrupt paths is what underlies the prophet's plea that the Israelites show loyalty for their Lord, and love and justice for each other. In the final segment of his book, chapters 13-14, Hosea reminds his contemporaries that "Israel's sin and guilt are on record, and the records are safely stored away" (13:12, Today's English Version). That is, past corruption is never forgotten either by human beings or by God. When sins are committed against an individual, those painful incidents are imprinted on memory banks, there to remain for life. Seemingly born with a kind of instant replay recorder built into all of us, our sufferings and heartaches, as well as our joys, are caught there and kept available for repeated reference. The replay mechanism can be tripped by any number of things. The name or sight of the person who hurt us, a similar incident experienced or mentioned, can cause that machine to go into operation! When it does we actually relive those blighted moments we have endured, with all of the old feelings of distress and resentment coming over us once more as though they were all happening on the spot at that instant.

The great problem the memory bank presents is that it cannot be stripped of its data. Even modern psychiatric procedures cannot eradicate the past in any selective and precise way. That is one of the reasons that where forgiveness is concerned the old proverb "Forget and forgive" at best is only partially possible. If we could forget we would not have to forgive, since the event that made forgiveness necessary could be eliminated, and that would be that!

It is because we remember, rather than forget, that we have to learn to forgive in spite of the past. Forgiveness is an act, as well as an attitude, which makes it possible for an offender to have a new chance to remake relationships despite the past which we both remember. Forgiveness is the quality in God and people which closes the files on the sins that have gone before and then locks them shut, treating a person as though they were newborn, even though we may have known them for a lifetime. Forgiveness focuses on the future possibilities for what the other person can become if given a new chance to begin again, not on the recounting of the shortcomings noted in the file which he or she may have demonstrated previously.

The Hebrew term for "remember," *zachar,* underlines this possibility. It means literally "to count," or "to recall." It is used by the psalmist when he pleads with the Lord to "remember not the sins of my youth" (Ps. 25:7), and by Isaiah when he pleads with God to "remember not iniquity forever" (Isa. 64:9). What both of these Old Testament saints were requesting was that rather than continually enumerating their errors of the past, God would never bring them up again, even though he, as well as they, had them printed indelibly upon their minds. This would give them the chance to begin a new chapter in life with the pages unstained and free.

That "heaven knows" how fallible we are is a far more accurate quip than some people imagine. What is equally beyond most people's comprehension is the great willingness of "heaven" to put aside the mental files on our demonstrated foolishness (13:13) and rebellion against the Lord (13:16) when we become truly repentant. In a sense, God is a gambler who is willing to place high stakes on the change-ability of human beings. A seemingly incurable optimist, the Lord regularly takes risks on those whose previous per-formance would make other people turn thumbs down on them for the future.

That is why the call for the chance for new life goes out to the people of Israel at the beginning of chapter 14 in the book of Hosea. The characteristic challenge of God through the prophets is sounded again, "Return to the Lord your God . . ." (14:1). The Hebrew word translated "return" is *shuv*. It usually is rendered in English either as "return" or "repent." Its root meaning is "to turn" or "to change direc-tion." The word anticipates a sharp shift in the direction in which a person is living his or her life.

Note that *shuv* includes activity as well as intentions. To *turn* anticipates people physically moving in paths diamet-rically opposed to the ones they had been walking. Repen-tance demands a change in life-style, as well as words of sorrow. As John the Baptist put it, sinners should "bear fruit that befits repentance" (Matt. 3:8; Luke 3:8). Such a reversal of both attitude and action was being asked for by the Lord of the nation when he challenged them to "return . . ." through the mouth of Hosea.

This does not mean that God's will to forgive was, or is, conditioned by our response to his mercy! He stands ready to give us new leases on life regardless of the previous attitudes we have lived out in our relationships with him or with each other. But note that the action of gift-giving can never be complete until the proffer of the gift is accepted by the potential recipient. You cannot hand a gift to another who continually turns his or her back on the treasure you are in the process of making available, even if the one doing the giving is God! To complete his act of forgiveness, we at God's prompting, and through the potential to do so which he lovingly built into us in the initial act of creation, must *shuv*, and turn around to face him and embrace his proffer. If that is done, the reconciliation God has longed for and labored to complete can take place. Then the prayer, and its attendant life-style, which Hosea outlines in 14:2-3, begins to become a reality. God once again moves into the center of the lives of those who once traded him off for what they thought were security and pleasure.

If that change Hosea prays for took place, then the way for a new era to begin was to be opened for his contemporaries (14:4-7). The nation would be enabled to "flourish like a garden and be fruitful like a vineyard" (14:7, TEV), with real prosperity for all. With such real changes of heart taking place, no veneer would be needed in an attempt to cover up a rotting social order, as was the case at the time Hosea was preaching to the northern kingdom. With God's help, a whole new society marked by justice and integrity would emerge, and a national calamity would be averted.

Hosea saw that the decision as to whether or not that would occur rested with the people, not with God. The Lord had continually pushed and pulled for reform in the individual and in the nation while they apparently had been determined to create their own future desolation. As his parting word through the prophecies of Hosea (14:9), God made it clear once more that he wanted to forgive rather than punish his people. If they were wise enough to act on the opportunity he was giving them for a new tomorrow, then all would be well for the future. If they refused, and ultimately were decimated, the tragedy that would strike them would be suicide, not divine murder. In either case, the next move was theirs!

With his sermons preached and his personal parable lived out, Hosea left for his people and for those of us who follow them his final admonition: "May those who are wise understand what is written here and take it to heart" (14:9, TEV).

5 AMOS:
JUDGMENT, JUSTICE, AND RENEWAL

The prophet Amos was a slightly older contemporary of Hosea. According to the kings listed in the preface of his book (Amos 1:1-2), Amos probably concluded his work about the time Hosea was reaching the zenith of his influence. Uzziah, the ruler of the southern kingdom, Judah, reigned from 783 to 746 B.C., and Jeroboam II ruled the north, or Israel, between 786 and 746 B.C. During the great majority of those years while Amos was active, prosperity was widespread, lulling the populace into a sense of complete security and a resulting complacency and moral corruption.

Although his home was in Tekoah, a fortified town about twelve miles south of Jerusalem, Amos' prophetic ministry was pointed essentially toward the northern kingdom. A common man whose occupation was that of a herdsman and caretaker of trees (7:14), he was sent by God to preach to the sophisticated people of the capital city of Samaria. For about a generation he delivered the messages which at one point aroused such hostility among some of the leaders of the realm that charges were brought against him to the king, and he was badgered to leave the area and go home (7:10-18). Unabashed, he continued his work, concluding his ministry sometime before that realm fell to the Assyrian conquerers in 721 B.C.

His prophecies reflected his background as a man familiar with the elements of nature and given to reflection. Common sights that other people might miss entirely contained for him messages from God (7:1-3, 4-6, 7-9; 8:1-3; 9:1-4). His oracles and sermons are conveyed in the straightforward speech of an unaffected human being. Often they fell like thunderclaps on the ears of those to whom euphemisms had become the norm.

The basic thrust of Amos' prophecies centered around his concern for social justice. The cry for fair treatment of the disadvantaged was the hallmark of most of the sermons he preached. Like the other prophets of Israel, for Amos religion was commitment lived out in day-to-day dealings with God and other human beings. Nothing else could replace morality and decency, not even the most pious religious ceremonies or costly sacrifices and offerings. It was the former, not the latter, that God demanded from his people. It was *justice now,* that God sent Amos to command his people to deliver!

The nations about whom Amos first prophesied are people that surrounded Israel. Syria (1:3-5) bordered it to the northeast, Philistia (1:6-8) occupied the plains to the west, the kingdom of Tyre (1:9-10) adjoined it to the immediate northwest, Edom (1:11-12) lay far to the south, separated from Israel by the southern kingdom of Judah, Ammon (1:13-15) bordered it beginning at the Jordan River to the east, Moab (2:1-3) encompassed the land south of Ammon, including in its territory much of the shore of the Dead Sea, and Judah, of course, adjoined Israel directly to the south, stretching from there to the wilderness called the Negeb. Taken together, the countries mentioned entirely enclosed Israel within their circle.

The common thread that describes the sins of these nations is that they were, each in their own ways, violating human beings individually, or en mass. God demanded a basic decency and reverence for life from *all* people, even from those who had not made the covenant with him such as Israel had at Sinai. Those who violated such commonly accepted norms came in for the Lord's judgment. Hence the prophet was called to speak against the nations who themselves were not part of the people the Lord had led out of slavery in Egypt to make peculiarly his own.

Against Judah (2:4-5) the charges were more sweeping than those made against the foreign countries. The peoples of the southern kingdom had "despised" the Lord's "teachings" and had not kept his "commands" which he had given them in the wilderness. What is more, they had embraced idolatry just as had some of their forebears. What made them so broadly condemned by Amos was that of all the other peoples named in his opening words of judgment, the people of Judah, as God's covenant partners, should have known better than to follow the corrupt paths they did. They, above all, should have lived out a sense of worth and dignity for all human beings in their dealings with each other. The people of Judah *knew* those commandments, indeed they had pledged themselves to obey them.

The most specific list of grievances God had Amos deliver were those he brought against Israel (2:6—3:2). Their chart of offenses reads like a manual for degrading the disadvantaged and helpless of society. Debtors were being sold into slavery when all they owed amounted to no more than the price of a pair of sandals (2:6). The defenseless and poor were being rolled over by those with more power and wealth than they had with which to secure their rights (2:7). Prostitution flourished as people used one another (2:7), apparently doing so in the name of God, so that worship places became both houses of prostitution and the countinghouses for usery, in both of which human values were playing second fiddle to "pleasure" (2:8).

What is appalling is that the ones perpetrating the sins were those who because of their commitment to the covenant made with God had been called to be the defenders of the underdog! They had once been slaves in Egypt themselves, whom God had freed from similar oppression and abuse. In fact, along the way to the Promised Land the Lord had counseled them to keep their past fixed firmly in mind (Exod. 22:21; 23:9), so that once they were free they would not do to others what once had been done to them.

What was shocking to both the Lord and Amos was how completely people can forget what oppression is like once the tables have been turned! The Israelites, like many others, before and after them, tended to duplicate with their children and their neighbors the painful indignities they

personally had experienced in their own past. What would
have been important for them to pull from their memories
was the fate suffered by the Egyptians for their oppression of
the Israelites. That also would have helped them to remember
the fact that their God had always taken the part of the
oppressed people in the world. Not only had that been true
for them, but it would always be true for those in their midst
who *then* were calling out for help. God had shown Israel in
his caring for them the same kind of compassion he had for
all people both in the ancient world and in our modern one.
When people suffer unjustly and cry out for help, the witness
of human history, particularly as it is recorded in the Bible, is
that God not only will hear but will respond to help liberate
and set them free. What was a shocking fact not only for the
Israelites in the time of Amos, but for many Judeo-Christian
societies in the centuries from then to now, is that very often
those of us who have been set free through the mercy of God
often become Pharaohs to others ourselves. In the face of
such oppression God always gets ready to act:

> For I know how many are your transgressions,
>   and how great are your sins—
> you who afflict the righteous, who take a bribe,
>   and turn aside the needy in the gate.
> Therefore he who is prudent will keep silent in such a time;
>   for it is an evil time.
> Seek good, and not evil,
>   that you may live;
> and so the Lord, the God of hosts, will be with you,
>   as you have said.
> Hate evil, and love good,
>   and establish justice in the gate;
> it may be that the Lord, the God of hosts,
>   will be gracious to the remnant of Joseph.
>
> (Amos 5:12-15)

For the prophets, all existence fitted together. There was a
reason for all things that occurred, and one of the organizing
forces in all of life was the hand of the Lord which was
actively participating day after day in shaping existence in
earthy, concrete ways. The prophets never "thought" of God
in abstract terms. He was a personal deity so close at hand
that he almost left his footprints in his world. While life

rolled on he was not off operating "out there" somewhere, detached from his creation. Quite the opposite. He was emeshed in the day-to-day goings-on in the lives of his people.

Sometimes the divine activity seemed directed largely toward the support and encouragement of the nation. The great Exodus experience, with its miraculous release from bondage, was an ever-remembered example of that. At other times, the divine hand seemed primarily to correct and discipline those same people when they grew corrupt. Both of these actions Amos perceived when he spoke the words recorded in chapters 3 through 9 of his book.

The God of Israel, while at times moved to anger, never was understood by the prophets as being capricious in any sense of that word. Judgment and destruction, when they came, were the just rewards for the sins of the people who were being weeded out by a long-suffering Creator. Even in such circumstances, however, God never acted without first giving adequate forewarnings (3:7). Amos, therefore, was prompted by God to proclaim to the nation the deluge which was going to come upon them, using as illustrations a series of metaphors drawn from the experiences of his hearers (3:2-6). These, apparently, were used to make the prophet's point because in his day and culture they would have been readily understood. Again, in a series of common sights which he saw while walking in the marketplace or in the fields, Amos found more divine messages to be wrapped up! Three of these visions held the ominous news that widespread misery was on its way for his countrymen. The sight of locusts swarming in the air conveyed the forecast of approaching devastation of the nation's food supply (7:1-2). Looking at a flame he was forewarned that a holocaust was going to sweep the land (7:4-6). A plumb line hanging next to a wall under construction (7:7-9) enabled the Lord to inform him of the divine distress over the crooked behavior of his people. Struck by the magnitude of what was to befall his contemporaries, Amos' response was to plead with God for forgiveness rather than punishment of the people (7:2, 5).

In the first two cases, the Lord answered the prophet's request by doing just what Amos had begged. Even though he had apparently already determined the response he wished to make to the nation's sinfulness, God reversed himself (in Hebrew, *nahim*, "to feel sorry") before actually implementing those designs.

Earlier (5:1—6:14) God had told the Israelites through Amos what was needed to avert such a personal and collective disaster. "Come to me, and you will live" was the plea Amos had been sent to make (5:4). "Work for what is right, not for what is evil . . . love good, see that justice prevails in the courts" (5:14-15). "Let justice flow like a stream and righteousness like a river that never goes dry" (5:24, TEV). For the onslaught to be averted something had to happen in the lives of the people! God was watching for a sign that they were willing to turn their lives around so that "justice" would become the norm for the realm. The term translated here "justice," in Hebrew, *mishpat*, meant "to give every person his or her rights and due." It involved the determination to treat people with absolute fairness, regardless of one's personal feelings about, or relationship to, the individual in question. Justice, in Hebrew, is always an active term, not simply a mental exercise. It is an attitude toward others that moves one to demonstrate love and respect with deeds of fair play and honesty. The person who receives such treatment did not have to bow and scrape for or because of it. In fact, those who received justice did not even have to offer thanks for it, since such treatment was theirs by *right*, being a creation of God. As such, their worth and dignity were to be respected by others, especially if those others had learned from the Lord the sanctity of all human life as the covenant entailed. No religious festival held (5:21) or material offering given (5:22) or hymns sung in ceremonial gatherings (5:24) could be substituted for this essential moral response. If such an ethical turnaround did not come from the populace, then whole armies would invade the land or natural catastrophies would strike, devastating the land from one end to the other (6:14; 7:1-5).

In the face of such ominous prospects, Amos prayed for a divine reprieve for his contemporaries. The word he employed when he cried out for God to "*forgive* your people, Lord!" (7:2) is *salach*. It is one of a number of Hebrew terms translated "forgive," or "forgiveness," in our English Bibles, each of which describes a different type of activity on the part of the person who does so. *Salach* essentially means "to send away," "to put distance between two people or objects." It is used to describe the act of forgiveness in which the sins a person has committed literally are taken and thrown or chased away from him or her forever. One of the ways that was symbolized in the Hebrew community in Amos' day was for the high priest to gather the nation together for a service of repentance and mourning. At one point in the liturgy the sins committed by all during the past year were confessed while the priest held his hands on the head of a goat, which later, as the bearer of the sins confessed over it, was driven out of the city gates into the wilderness to be slain. The killing of this "scapegoat" was a visual reminder that, as the animal, the sins confessed over it could be laid to rest too. It was a sign to the nation that God did the same with the guilt of the people once they were willing to truly confess it. In a very real way, the ceremony was a simple drama of how God dealt with his own wayward children (see Lev. 4:20; Ps. 8:5; 103:3).

Another common term for "forgiveness" is *caphar* (see Ps. 78:38; Jer. 18:23). Literally, it means "to cover over" or "to fill in," usually referring to a hole that is stopped up with a substance of some kind. It is a builder's term often employed by those engaged in ship construction (see Gen. 6:14), where it refers to the practice of caulking the hull of a boat, that is, filling in the gaps between the boards to enable a vessel filled with holes to float and function as it was designed to do. Scribes also used the term, referring to their method for correcting errors in their written texts. Since in early times writing was done primarily on clay tablets, other material having not yet been developed, mistakes in a line made by a writer could not be erased as simply as they are now. When

such a miscue occurred, the scribe obliterated it by filling in
the indentation he had made with a small pinch of new clay
taken from his pot. Pressing it into the hole made in the
tablet, with his moistened finger he would smooth over the
surface, making it ready for a new word.

A third term usually translated "forgiveness" is *nasah* (see
Gen. 50:17; Ps. 32:2). Its root meaning is "to lift up," "to
lift away," or "to stand on one's feet." When used to describe a situation in which forgiveness is taking place, it points
to the activity of removing a burden from the back of a
heavily-laden person, or helping an individual who has fallen
to the ground to stand on his or her feet in an upright
position again.

Note that in each instance forgiveness involves an activity
as well as an attitude. Forgiveness, like love, flows from
persons to persons in concrete demonstrations of shielding
the present from the past, lifting away heavy loads, and
enabling a human being to function freely again. When Amos
pleads with the Lord "to forgive Israel" (Amos 7:2), his
request has such implications attached to it. He is asking the
Lord to withhold the calamity he intends to send, giving the
people a chance for a "clean" future instead.

As usual, God was willing to answer the prophet's request.
"The Lord changed his mind and said, 'What you saw will not
take place' " (7:3, 6). Thousands of times he had done the
same thing in the past, hoping on every occasion that his
people would use their new starts with him in positive ways.
Unfortunately, that did not happen where the northern
kingdom was concerned. What they chose to do was to
remain "crooked" rather than plumb (7:8), using the.oppor-
tunity the Lord's forgiveness had given to multiply their sins.
Therefore, in 722-721 B.C., the judgment which the Lord
had threatened on the northern kingdom came when the
Assyrian army invaded the land and utterly destroyed it,
carrying many of its citizens off into exile.

Those who had trampled the needy (8:4), cheated in the
marketplace (8:5ff.), and enslaved people for the price of a
pair of sandals (8:6) got their due. The Lord had warned that

he would "shake the people of Israel like grain in a sieve" and "shake them among the nations to remove all who were worthless" (9:9). That he did! However, from the divine sifting some were to be saved, since not "all the descendants of Jacob" would be destroyed (9:8). At least a remnant would remain which God would then use to form a more faithful people for the future. Of this ultimate reformation and renewal Amos was as convinced as he was that God would never ignore evil and let it win the day.

It is this unsinkable love of God which repeatedly kept him from obliterating his creation that comes through at the conclusion of Amos' prophecies (9:11-15). Even though the people had rejected God's attempts to save them, the Lord tells Amos again that one day the land will be regained, its towns rebuilt, and the people who are going to be scattered brought back to inhabit both. When that happened it would all be God's doing, another gift he was planning to give out of his seemingly endless generosity. He informed his prophet, "*I will repair . . . I will rebuild . . . I will bring my people back to their land . . .*," making it plain that he was not going to desert for eternity the people he must punish. The land that was to be burned and covered with corpses one day would become a garden spot where life would appear again. God promised *that* even *before* the fury of the punishment that was to come! With that note Amos ended his prophecy, apparently to speak no more. One can imagine that he must have shaken his head upon receiving such a divine commitment that so unspeakable a tragedy looming ahead had to be caused by human recalcitrance when the gift being readied for the future could have been theirs on the spot!

6 MICAH: RIGHTEOUSNESS AND OBEDIENCE

The city of Moresheth, or Mareshah, from which the prophet Micah came, is situated in the rolling lowlands about twenty miles southwest of Jerusalem. If modern archeologists are correct, the village lies near the ancient Philistine city of Gath. According to the introduction of the book, Micah prophesied during the reigns of Jotham (750-735 B.C.), Ahaz (735-715 B.C.), and Hezekiah (715-687 B.C.)—all monarchs of the southern kingdom of Judah. He was, therefore, a contemporary of both Hosea and Amos. While the other two prophets had the northern kingdom as a focus for their ministries, Micah's labors were confined primarily to Judah, with scattered references to Samaria found here or there in his prophecies. Even though they spent their lives in different parts of the land, it is surprising that Micah never refers to the words of either of his contemporaries and that neither Hosea nor Amos mentions him. Nevertheless, the common threads that linked these three prophets together become readily apparent in even a quick comparison of their books.

The bulk of Micah's prophecies appear to come after the destruction of the northern kingdom which took place in 721 B.C. The major thrust of his prophecies formed themselves around the same types of problems that caused the downfall of the northern kingdom, namely, the oppression of the weak in society by a leadership which benefited from the exploitation of the poor of the land. Like the other eighth-century prophets, Micah saw such behavior as a sign of moral decadence. Such oppression of the weak was glaring evidence that faithfulness to the covenant which the nation had made with the Lord had totally collapsed. His mission, therefore, was to call them to repentance in a change of life-style, and to warn his countrymen of dire consequences should they fail to reform themselves and the social order.

The cause for Micah's lament of the nation's waywardness (Mic. 1:2–3:12) is now familiar to us after having dealt earlier with the books of Hosea and Amos. His opening prophetic statement takes the form of the *riv* or prophetic lawsuit made against Judah. Like a prosecuting attorney facing an offender in court, God speaks through Micah to press his case against his people, indicting them for rebellion against him (1:5), the most serious sin of which any person or group could be guilty. Idols had been set up in the land (1:7) which God had graciously given to his children for a home. The Lord had been replaced with objects of wood and stone to which the people who had come through the Exodus with him were now giving their allegiance. Such practices, which they had adopted from their pagan neighbors, inevitably had tied up with them moral structures and life-styles which were repugnant to the Lord of Israel.

One of the chief aberrations being practiced by the people was the stealing of land and homes from their rightful owners (2:2, 9). Such an act, next to murder, was one of the most serious crimes one could perpetrate against another (see 1 Kings 21:1ff.). Not only did it deprive an individual of the value of his holdings, but it in fact broke up one of the keys to family solidarity and identity. In the ancient east, land and houses were part of a birthright passed on from a father to his heirs. Land and houses were, as they still are for many Arabs in that section of the world today, carriers of the family's history and name. They were a home base to which the family could return in times of need or trial. They signified the spots where a person's parents, and their parent's parents before them, had been born, labored, and finally died, caring for as well as being cared for by the plots of earth in which they laid buried. A sense of permanence and continuity, a security and independence, developed between families and the soil. A sense of *being* was bound up with the ground and the developments that had been erected upon it.

To rob someone of his or her money was to violate his person. But to take away a person's land was to steal a very part of his history and identity.

Justice everywhere was being perverted in the social structure (Mic. 3:1). The legal system, which was supposed to provide fair treatment and equality for all, was being used to subjugate those with the fewest defenses for themselves. Bribes were being paid (3:11). People were being trampled by vicious connivers who seemed to operate without restraint. Such a condition made for a disastrous situation in a land which had no police forces, as such, to protect persons from social abuse. Taking care of "kin" was the responsibility of a person's family or of an indentured servant by his or her master. When an individual was stripped of such assistance through death or distance, or by being destitute, the judicial system was supposed to be the one place to which they could turn for humane treatment at times of jeopardy. When such was no longer the case, a situation arose where all people were threatened because eventually they might find themselves alone, hounded by grabbers and finaglers.

Moreover, the religious and civil leaders of the southern kingdom were individually and corporately corrupted as well, and were being called to account by Micah for their part in the problems that were rampant. They were the ones who by office and training had the responsibility to keep the nation on an even keel. But both apparently had sold out, or been bought up, in one way or another. They added to the problem instead of being a part of the potential solution. Prophets lied and peddled promises of prosperity or doom depending on the ability and willingness of those who were consulted to pay for their oracles (2:11; 3:5). Money "talked" from one end of society to the other for those who had it. But what all of the leaders, prophets or princes, forgot was that the Lord had ears to hear the "conversation" which they in their wealth were carrying on! What is more, when the Lord got the message he moved through Micah to respond to it! Just as the sins of the north had brought destruction to Samaria (1:9), the same was predicted to happen to Judah in Jerusalem (1:9). Going naked and bare-foot through the streets of Jerusalem to dramatize his message in a form of "multimedia," Micah delivered a fateful prophecy to the inhabitants of the nation's capital. To their startled ears came the thunderous proclamation: " . . . Zion will be plowed like a field, Jerusalem will become a pile of ruins, and the temple hill will become a forest" (3:12).

Despite his best efforts at driving his point home, the people of his day refused to respond to the preaching of Micah. They also found it incredible that there was any possibility of the divine patience wearing thin. What may have helped make the people respond to Micah's oracle with disbelief was the words they had been getting from the pandering prophets prior to his coming. They had been promising support for the policies and practices going on, providing assurance that God was at ease and satisfied with life as it was (2:11; 3:5). When they were confronted by a prophet of a different stripe with other allegiances, *he* was the one whose word they were willing to discount.

Like many of the true prophets of God, Micah was not the only one who had to contend with such a predicament. Yet he alone among those on the scene was able to see with clarity what the true situation and state of the nation was. Prodded by his perceptions, he was moved to speak the truth regardless of the consequences. With courage supplied by the Lord (3:8), he continued to call a spade a spade, even if the delivering of the sermons frightened and hurt the people he confronted. His willingness to do so, rather than being a sign of vindictiveness, was actually a clue to the great love he held for his people. That love made it impossible for him to watch them die without making an attempt to rescue them.

The love and evenhandedness of God was never doubted by Micah. Even in his moments of greatest wrath what Micah saw the Lord doing was simply giving his people what they deserved! Even *those* occasions came only after all else had failed. God usually tried softer and more tender ways to deal with his nation. Long series of warnings, and often pleadings, preceded any pain-bringing interventions. That was true in the days preceding the destruction of both the northern and then the southern kingdoms.

In an almost last-ditch attempt to avert the destruction of Judah, God again pleaded his case against her, outlining the ways she had open to avoid the imminent disaster. The Lord began by enumerating the events from the nation's history which demonstrated how far he had gone to save and assist his people at important junctures in their lives. As he did so, God called on nature itself, that is, the mountains and the "foundations of the earth" (6:2), to listen to his case, acting as a jury in the proceedings.

The Lord opened his case by recalling the greatest of all saving events he performed for the Israelites, the Exodus experience through which he freed them from Egyptian bondage (6:3-4). He followed that (6:5a) by reminding them of how when Balak, king of Moab, tried to employ Balaam, a Mesopotamian diviner, who lived at Pethro, a town near Carchemish, to put a curse on the Israelites while they were in the process of invading the land, the Lord sent his angel to stop him from doing so (Num. 22:1—24:25). He goes on (Mic. 6:5b) to refresh their memories about how he had dried up the waters of the Jordan River in a second "sea crossing," when it loomed as a barrier to his people's entry into the Promised Land as they moved toward Gilgal under Joshua's leadership (Josh. 3—4). All of these were wondrous events which no human being could have accomplished. The Lord had done them all to save the nation, giving it its freedom as well as a country in which to live that freedom out, all through his generosity!

As a response to that mercy and love, God did not ask for burnt offerings (6:6), the gifts of sheep or oil, or the sacrifices of children (6:7). What he had requested from his people was the following of the life-style which he had shown them would be "good," in Hebrew, *tov*, "shaped according to God's pleasure and design." That shape or design was quite simple in its requirements: "To do what is just, show constant love, and humbly obey our God" (6:8).

The requirement of justice, in Hebrew, *mishpat*, as pointed out in our discussion of the prophecy of Amos, meant "to give every person his or her rights and due." It had at its heart the necessity of treating people with complete fairness, regardless of one's personal feelings about, or relationship to, the people in question. .

Hesed was expected by God from his people as well. Often translated "constant love," "steadfast love," or "unending love," this Hebrew term actually means "a dogged, determined, unwilling-to-let-go, unable-to-wear-out, won't-say-quit kind of love"! No single English word can capture it completely. It is a term all wrapped up with a covenant relationship between God and Israel in which each promises lifelong loyalty to the other. *Hesed* expresses a determination to live out that commitment through thick or thin, better or worse, for richer or for poorer. As such, it carried within it the expectation from God that his people would "hang in there" with him and each other, practicing with him and other human beings the qualities of life he had taught them through his dealings with them over the ages.

"Humble obedience" was assumed by God from his people, too. *Zanah*, the Hebrew word that stands behind that English rendering, means "to keep up," "to stay in step," with another person with whom one happens to be walking and who is setting the pace for the journey. It does not mean to walk with one's head hanging in an attitude of the beaten spirit. It has no atmosphere of subjugation about it. Rather, it depicts a person who with a springy step is hustling to match a rate of travel that she or he might find a challenge!

What *zanah* was asking from the people of Judah was that they act toward God and their compatriots with the same love and concern the Lord had shown them. "Match me, step for step, style for style in our relationship," is what God was saying to Israel through the mouth of Micah. Yahweh was not a Lord who demanded that people do what they were told by him. He always asked that they do as he *did*, patterning their lives after his own. When he called them "my people," and they answered him "my God," cementing the covenant, they had entered into an intimate bond with him that linked each to the other. Henceforth, they were to follow in his moral and ethical footsteps throughout their lives.

Lives that were patterned in such a way were characterized by "righteousness." In Hebrew, *tzedekah*, the word usually translated into English as "righteousness," means "to *do* what is right," "to *act* appropriately." Righteousness was something one *did*, not just a thought he or she had about a person specifically or generally! It was *caring* acted out in nuts-and-bolts, person-to-person relationships. The Hebrews and God were well aware of the fact that what is in a person's heart inevitably will appear in his or her life-style. As Jesus was later to say: "Are grapes gathered from thorns, or figs from thistles? So, every sound tree bears good fruit, but the bad tree bears evil fruit. . . . Thus you will know them by their fruits." (Matt. 7:16-17, 20)

It is interesting to note that where the Bible uses the term "righteousness" to describe individuals, they are always engaged in *living out* God's will for them, or are caught up in *acts* of compassion for other human beings. Noah, for instance, was designated a *tzadik,* or righteous man, because he was "blameless in his generation; Noah walked with God" (Gen. 6:9). That is, God set the pace by which Noah shaped his own life, which is what God through Micah was calling the people of his day to do (Mic. 6:8c). Abram "believed the Lord; and he reckoned it to him as righteousness" (Gen. 15:6). In Hebrew the term we translate in this passage "believed" comes from the Hebrew word *emunah*. It means essentially "to stand firm," "to hang in." It depicts a person who has pressure exerted upon him or her to be pushed off balance or out of a path in which he or she is walking. It implies active effort being made to stay on the line or maintain one's balance. Hence, faithfulness or "belief" is something that one does, not something that one simply possesses like a coin grasped with the hand. Proverbs 10:1ff. in depicting the activities of the righteous man tells us that he "walks in integrity," "heeds instruction," etc. In each case, their existence is shaped along the lines God marked out as being proper.

Such behavior Micah declared to be "wise" (Mic. 6:9). Its opposite was not only foolish but ultimately disastrous, bringing "ruin and destruction" (6:11), as Omri and his son Ahab, kings of the northern realm (1 Kings 16:25ff.), learned. If they chose to follow suit despite God's generous acts in saving and sustaining them in the past, and his pleadings and efforts to turn them from their increasingly corrupt ways in the present, then the people of Judah were giving God no other option than to throw up his hands and declare, "It is hopeless! . . . There is not an honest man left in the land, no one loyal to God" (Mic. 7:1a, 2a).

That is precisely what the headstrong people seemed determined to do. Their course apparently settled, the day for their punishment was one that Micah saw looming just over the horizon. Apparently all alone among the people of Judah in his desire to serve his God, Micah probably shook his head as he turned away saying, "But *I* will watch for the Lord. *I* will wait confidently for God, who will save me. My God *will* hear me" (7:7).

As with nearly all of the prophets, God's parting words to his people through Micah were ones of hope and future restoration. The same One who had predicted that "Zion will be plowed like a field, Jerusalem will become a pile of ruins, and the temple hill will become a forest" (3:12), told the nation that would endure the catastrophe, "People of Jerusalem, the time to rebuild the city walls is coming. At that time your territory will be enlarged. Your people will return to you from everywhere . . ." (7:11-12). Even through the clouds of the gathering storm the compassion of God again shined!

Micah himself banked on that character of God holding firm for the future. The final seven verses of his book are a prayer to the Lord to remain the shepherd of his people, to lead them through the "wilderness" into which they had strayed (7:14). He asks for another series of "mighty works," similar to what had happened in the Exodus (7:15) to free his countrymen from their self-imposed bondage. Forgiveness would be necessary for that to take place, but he was convinced that God would not "stay angry forever" (7:18). The

divine mercy would again show itself, and God's faithfulness
and *hesed* would "hand in" (7:20). Since the Lord had
promised the descendants of Abraham that he would relate
to them as such a God, and since he had proved to them
constantly through the ages that his word and promises were
good, Micah, at least, could face the future with confidence.
For, with God standing by, his people could endure any
disaster without utter despair. Beyond the suffering they
would encounter, he would be waiting to embrace them
anew.

7 JEREMIAH: SALVATION AND FAITHFULNESS

Few prophets have lived during a period of more history-shaping events than did Jeremiah. The four decades of his ministry (ca. 626-585 B.C.) encompassed the collapse of the world-dominating Assyrian empire (612 B.C.), the power struggle between Egypt under Pharaoh Necho and Babylonia, led by King Nebuchadnezzar, to take over the dominance previously held by Assyria, and the defeat of Egypt by the Babylonians and the Medes in 605 B.C. that made the former the masters of the Near East for slightly more than a half-century.

During these violent years Jeremiah lived through the experience of having his own nation, a key buffer state between the competing world powers, go from being in subjugation to Assyria, to national independence and freedom, to near total destruction with most of her population, and nearly all of her leaders, carried off into exile. Amidst the swirl of these events, Jeremiah prayed, spoke, struggled, wept, threatened, and pleaded with his contemporaries and God to effect a revolution in faith and morality among the people of Judah which could keep his nation from the destruction he saw approaching for it.

Jeremiah was born in the village of Anathoth (modern Anata), located about three-and-one-half miles northeast of Jerusalem. It is a town about one hour's distance from the capital on foot. While the actual date of his birth is not known, it seems likely to have been about 645-640 B.C., making him between fourteen and nineteen years of age when he began his prophetic ministry, probably in 626 B.C. Jeremiah was the son of Hilkiah, a priest from the line of

Abiathar, the high priest of King David, who was banished to
Anathoth by Solomon for supporting Adonijah in his revolt
against him (1 Kings 2:26-28). Although he came from this
priestly line and was trained in their sacred literature and
customs, there is no evidence that Jeremiah ever functioned
as a priest in the temple in Jerusalem.

Jeremiah began his ministry clearly perceiving himself as a
prophet of God. He understood himself to have been fore-
ordained by the Lord for the task:

> Before I formed you in the womb I knew you, and before you
> were born I consecrated you; I appointed you a prophet to the
> nations (Jer. 1:4-5).

Even though he preached during the reigns of five Judean
kings, three of whom are named in the prologue of his book,
Josiah (640-609 B.C.), Jehoiakim (609-597 B.C.), and
Zedekiah (597-586 B.C.), and two others who may have been
omitted from the list because each ruled for only three
months, Jehoahaz (609 B.C.) and Jehoiachin (597 B.C.), and
related to some of them face-to-face, Jeremiah never forgot
Who it was who called him to prophesy or Who it was to
whom he ultimately was accountable.

The record of Jeremiah's relationship with God in chapters
10 through 20 of his book is one of the great treasures of the
Bible. An extremely sensitive, "feeling," and perceptive man,
he often was torn internally by the positions of conflict and
alienation in which his prophetic role frequently placed him
vis-à-vis his contemporaries. A tender and perhaps shy person,
Jeremiah was called by Yahweh to oppose kings, princes,
priests, other prophets, and ultimately nearly all of his countrymen before he died. A person who longed for warm
human relationships, he was told by God that he would have
to give up hopes for a family of his own (16:1-2) for a life of
isolation and "nay-saying." So lonely and alienated did he become that at times he raged against God for having fingered
him out for a divine call! At one point in his life, when his
loneliness reached its zenith, he screamed that God had violated his very being in order to force him into his service. The
Revised Standard Version of the Bible records the outcry:

> O Lord, thou hast *deceived* me,
>   and I was deceived;
> thou art *stronger* than I,
>   and thou hast prevailed.
>   (20:7, italics added)

Such a translation is far too weak a rendering of the Hebrew text, which more accurately reads:

> O Lord, you have *seduced* me,
>   and I was seduced;
> you have *raped* me,
>   and I was overpowered.

The two key Hebrew verbs italicized above are *patah*, in the first case, and *hazak* in the second. *Patah* is used in the Bible to describe the act of enticing a person into premarital sexual intercourse (Exod. 22:16; Hos. 2:12; Job 31:9). *Hazah* means to force with violence, against her will, a woman into sexual intercourse. What Jeremiah is accusing God of is first *luring* him, then *forcing* his will upon him, to do his bidding at high personal cost to his servant! So painful was that call to the prophetic ministry that at times Jeremiah wished he had never been born, or had died immediately thereafter (20:14-18).

Not all of his life was lived in such misery, however. There were times when his relationship with Yahweh was one of joy, delight, and supreme support. The same prophet who could wail about God's seduction of him was the same one who could say:

> Thy words were found, and I ate them,
>   and thy words became to me a joy
>   and the delight of my heart;
> for I am called by thy name,
>   O Lord, God of Hosts.
>   (15:16)

These internal struggles kept Jeremiah in close and continual communion with God throughout his lifetime. Although the "lovers quarrels" do not seem to have found their way into his public utterances, Jeremiah repeated them to his faithful scribe, Baruch, enabling him to preserve them for future generations as a diary that showed the unfolding and growth in faith of one of the greatest of God's prophets. He also has helped millions of others of us to understand and plumb the depths and heights of our own religious commitment and development by peering into his heart and life.

Jeremiah, at the same time he was God's spokesman, was also the prophet of the people. Even when he met with sharp opposition from those to whom he preached, he continued to intercede for them with God until ordered by the Lord to cease and desist (7:16; 11:14; 14:11). This he did even though at various points his countrymen flogged him and put him in the stocks overnight (20:1ff.), forced him into hiding (36:27ff.; 37:11ff.), tried and imprisoned him as a traitor (32:1ff.), and threw him into a mud-filled cistern and left him there to smother in its slime (38:6ff.). To the very end of his ministry he continued to love with a passion the ones to whom he most often had to preach messages of doom and impending disaster.

The nation Jeremiah confronted had become so morally decadent and corrupt following the years of rule by King Manasseh (687-642 B.C.) that not even his grandson Josiah's desperate effort at reforming and reconsecrating nearly every facet of national and personal life in his revival beginning in 621 B.C. (2 Kings 22:1ff.) was able to turn his realm lastingly in a new direction. In his famous Temple Sermon, Jeremiah agonized over the corruption of his people:

> Behold, you trust in deceptive words to no avail. Will you steal, murder, commit adultery, swear falsely, burn incense to Baal, and go after other gods that you have not known, and then come and stand before me in this house, which is called by my name, and say, "We are delivered!"—only to go on doing all these abominations? Has this house, which is called by my name, become a den of robbers in your eyes? Behold, I myself have seen it, says the Lord. (7:8-11)

Instead of heeding his persistent warnings over the many years of his prophetic ministry, the leaders and populace grew so recalcitrant that finally Jeremiah lost faith in the potential of his people to revamp their styles of life. As though throwing up his hands in utter despair, he told them:

> Can the Ethiopian change his skin
>   or the leopard his spots?
> Then also you can do good
>   who are accustomed to do evil.
> I will scatter you like chaff
>   driven by the wind from the desert.
> This is your lot,
>   the portion I have measured out to you, says the Lord. . . .
>   (13:23 25)

The "scattering" of his people occurred, in fact, in 598-597 B.C. and 587-586 B.C., when in successive invasions the Babylonian king Nebuchadnezzar conquered the land, carrying off in his first trip its leaders into exile and returning a decade later to destroy the villages of the country and Jerusalem itself in an attempt to annihilate the rebellious Israelites who schemed and plotted to throw off his domination (2 Kings 24—25). When the capital city was taken in 586 B.C., the leader of the Babylonian troops that put Jerusalem to the torch, Nebuzaradan, gave Jeremiah, who had for years counseled the kings of his land to submit to Babylonian rule, the option of going with him to Babylon and living there in security or remaining in his homeland, which at that very moment was in flames before his eyes (Jer. 40:1-6). True to his lifelong commitment to his countrymen, Jeremiah chose the latter, preferring to share the lot of the people he loved so passionately despite their callousness and rejection of him.

Amidst the flames, Jeremiah predicted that the day would come when God would again bring his people back to the Promised Land where they would once more live in peace and tranquillity with Him and each other (chs. 30-34). Jeremiah himself did not live to see that occur. Instead, following another revolt in which the Babylonian-appointed governor, Gedaliah, was assassinated by a group of rebels led by Ishmael, a member of the Judean royal family (Jer. 41:1-3; 2 Kings 25:25), Jeremiah was carried off by the insurrectionists who took him with them when they fled to Egypt for sanctuary (Jer. 43:6-7). There he apparently died, unheeded by those he was sent to help save from destruction, but faithful to the One who had appointed him as his prophet! He stands today as one of the greatest spokesmen of God, the one who supremely embodied faithfulness to his Lord, love for his people, and courage in the face of adversity, not only calling for a practice of individual and national piety, but as Jesus was later to do supremely, demonstrating with his own body and resources what such faith looks like in action in the here and now.

A theme that rings throughout the book of Jeremiah like a bell clanging through the night is that of the hope of salvation for his nation. From warnings and laments proclaiming that the opportunity for salvation seems to be slipping away (8:20), to prayers spoken to God that it may yet occur (14:7-9), to assurances that it in fact will happen in God's good time (30:10, 11), Jeremiah employed the term more than twenty times in various forms and contexts. The way he uses the term, as well as the way it is expressed throughout most of the Scriptures of the Old and New Testaments alike, may be surprising to many who look closely at the texts where the word is employed. The surprise that usually comes from such close scrutiny of the biblical material usually is based on finding that salvation in the biblical sense has more to do with the here and now than it does with life in the "there" and the "hereafter"! What makes it so is that for many Christians whose modes of thought have been largely developed by the patterns of the Western world, salvation is a term that has had its primary focus and emphasis on what happens to a person after birth rather than on what is in store for us after the embalmer gets us!

To the Hebrews, however, salvation had its primary, though not only, emphasis on that segment of life we experience before death. Jeremiah's pleadings and admonitions usually have to do with sparing the nation from destruction or the ultimate restoration of his people in their own homeland within history, not at the end of it. Indeed, the term we translate into English as "salvation" is *yashah*. In its root sense, *yashah* is a builder's term that means simply "to make spacious," "to set free," or "to push back the walls." Like the Greek term used in the New Testament for the same experience, *soteria*, it has as its goal the freeing up of people from situations or individuals who threaten to hem them in, annihilate them, or take away their freedom. Salvation is not something merely "spiritual," but refers to a condition that takes into account a person's material, present problems as well as the future he or she might have in the next world. When Jeremiah employs the term it is always in this orthodox or *traditional* frame of reference. When the Hebrew slaves were dashing away from their mudpits in Egypt toward the land of freedom promised to them by God, and became trapped by the pursuing Egyptian army at the edge of the sea, and "the Lord *saved* Israel that day out of the hands of their enemies" (Exod. 14:30), what was clearly meant in the original text was that God saved them *from* death not *after* it! When David "saved the inhabitants of Keilah" from the attacking Philistines (1 Sam. 23), he did so by setting them free from their adversaries and giving them the opportunity to live in freedom and safety. In nearly every other instance where the term *yashah* appears it has this "contemporary," immediate action in mind. The prophets continued, by and large, to see that salvation had to do with individuals as total beings, whose lives were in every area in need of God's "freeing up," "liberating" activity. When God tells Isaiah to

> bring good tidings to the afflicted . . . bind up the brokenhearted . . . proclaim liberty to the captives . . . and open the eyes of the blind (Isa. 61:1)

he was pointing to salvation including, but not being limited to, very physical things.

We ought not to be surprised, then, to find Jesus' own teaching about salvation reflecting the same emphasis. Throughout his ministry he cared for the physical as well as the spiritual needs of those who came to him. His first acts when he returned from his forty days of retreat in the wilderness were to go on a mission of healing as well as preaching. From that point onward the "material" and "spiritual" aspects of existence were rolled into one ball of wax!

What is important for us to keep in mind in understanding

the preaching of Jeremiah and the other prophets and writers of the Scriptures is the fact that the Bible tells us that the God who saves includes in this work justice and loving care for people here and now as well as making provisions for that dimension of life that carries beyond the grave. Moreover, God calls us to have the same commitment when *we* work to bring the reality of salvation to those we meet.

Just as God does in his efforts, when we act to move a brother or sister into a "saved" relationship with Him, we must focus on life after birth as well as on life after death. Such a biblical thrust will not allow us to get into a neat little detached-from-reality tie-up with the Lord, saying, "Now its *you* and *me*, God, right? It's just you and me!" while all around us people are suffering from situations and needs we could well help remedy and satisfy.

If one is going to use the term "salvation" as the prophets and Bible do, we will have to be interested in the material problems of the world as well as in the spiritual dimensions of human existence. To be interested in the salvation of human beings in this biblical sense will push us to be interested in such here and now things as open housing, the liberation of oppressed peoples, and the freeing up of human beings from whatever may dehumanize and depersonalize them. While it will keep us ever mindful that there is more to life than bread alone, it will prevent us from backing another human being into a corner asking, "Are you saved?" and then leaving him or her to answer that question while suffering through life alone. Being concerned about salvation in a prophetic sense calls us to stand with human beings in the midst of all the complex challenges and pains of living, and, with God's help, enable them to see the Lord's concern for them in the midst of all they are experiencing. It will help us see that the love of God which goes on into eternity wraps itself around every moment and area of our lives including the present one.

Two of the sharpest indictments made of his contemporaries by Jeremiah was that they had both forsaken God and turned a deaf ear to his pleadings to recommit themselves to him (2:1ff.). In a pungent sermon preached at the gate of the Temple in Jerusalem (7:1-15), the prophet laid out the specifics of the moral corruption that attended that break with the Lord. Almost as an epilogue to that address he caught up the dilemma in a nutshell:

> This is the nation that did not obey the voice of the Lord their God, and did not accept *discipline; truth* has perished; it is cut off from their lips (7:28).

The Hebrew text that stands behind the translation of this verse in the Revised Standard Version of the Bible is much more vivid than its English rendering. The term which appears in our translation as "discipline" in Hebrew, *musar*, means "to take instruction," "to accept guidance." It depicts an individual, in this instance God, trying patiently and persistently to guide a person in a positive direction, or teach a valuable lesson, which the individual, in this case an entire nation, resists no matter how caringly and lovingly the attempt is being made. Stubbornness, not lack of capacity to learn, is the root of the problem.

The word translated "truth" is the Hebrew *emunah,* whose basic emphasis is somewhat different from the English term employed. In its root sense *emunah* means "to stand firm," "to hang in," or "to hold one's position." The word can best be illustrated by a person who is holding on to the end of a rope for dear life while another is trying to pull it out of her or his hands, or an individual who is trying to stand on a mark or given point while others are trying to push him over or off of his position. Like most Hebrew words it is a term describing an *activity* experienced in real life situations. *Emunah* could be more accurately translated into our idiom as "faithfulness." Such a rendering catches up the sense of acting in loyalty, one with another, that the R.S.V. does not convey. The term "truth" employed in the R.S.V. can be abstract and impersonal by contrast, something *emunah* never is. Faithful *activity* was a quality that God continually called for from his covenant partners. Love of their Lord, as well as faithfulness to each other, involved performance that demonstrated the value each had for the other.

God demonstrated such faithfulness time and again in his relationship with his people. After he lovingly created the first human beings he supplied them with a planet to inhabit, and help for his newly-fashioned creatures in developing their potential as co-creators with their Maker (Gen. 1:28). After sin bent their own lives and the created order that surrounded them out of shape, God still "stood firm" beside them, providing clothing made with his own hands as "paradise" ended, at least for the time being (Gen. 3:20). Later still when the Israelites were mired in Egyptian slavery God "hung in" with them. He led them out of bondage, rolling back a sea for their safe passage into a land where they could exercise their freedom once again. God *acted out* his commitment to his people in concrete ways. He continually expected them to do likewise!

In the preaching of Jeremiah the call for such a response is made by God: "*Turn around*, O faithless sons, I will heal your faithlessness" (3:22). Through Hosea, God reminds the nation: "What I want from you is plain and clear: I want your *constant* love . . . I would rather have my people '*know me*' than give burnt offerings to me" (Hos. 6:5-6, TEV). Paul later was to call for "faith working through love" (Gal. 5:6). Each of the spokesmen for the Lord held up the necessity for actions on the part of all of us that make our faith come alive as the shaper of our life styles.

Faithfulness, in the biblical sense, always means involvement with God's creation in both its human and inanimate forms. It involves showing real, active concern for people who are hungry, alienated, hurt, denied the basic rights and freedoms and dignity God meant for us all. It calls us to involvement with changing things that cause such suffering and human degradation, even when working for such change is unpopular and gets personally expensive. Moreover, it asks for us to work for such changes where you and I live, as well as for such revision by people and places half the world away.

Faithfulness always involves keeping a sharp ear, eye, and

heart open to the call of God in every dimension of our existence. It pushes us to cooperate with him in the healing of his world by keeping in constant intimate and personal touch with him who placed us in it at the beginning! The ways that God may make his approach to touch us individually will vary from person to person and from moment to moment. It may be that his use of a variety of contacts is meant to keep us on our toes and sensitive to his presence at all times and places. What he desires from each is that we remain close to him, hanging in through good times as well as bad ones, through joy as well as suffering from the moment of consciousness through the day of resurrection. By moving through life with such real togetherness we may thus develop into the kind of persons and human family where the love and concern and compassion of the creator become the hallmarks of those he made.

8 EZEKIEL: PUNISHMENT AND RESURRECTION

Like the great prophet Jeremiah, who was an older contemporary, Ezekiel fulfilled his ministry at a time of national
catastrophe. Called by the Lord to preach to the nation just
prior to its conquest by Nebuchadnezzar, the great Babylonian king, in 598-597 B.C., this son of Buzi and a descendant
from a line of priests (Ezek. 1:3) had the house he possessed
left empty by the death of his wife (24:18), faced the awesome task of delivering messages of impending doom to a
multitude of contemporaries who turned deaf ears to his persistent warnings, and later himself was carried into exile
during the calamity that fell upon them during his lifetime.
His was a "pressure-cooker" ministry in every sense of the
term!

The "call" to the prophetic ministry itself was a dramatic
one for Ezekiel. In a moment of ecstasy/vision Yahweh
marked him out as his personal spokesman to Israel in a
unique ceremony:

> And he said to me, "Son of man, eat what is offered to you; eat
> this scroll, and go, speak to the house of Israel." So I opened my
> mouth and he gave me the scroll to eat. And he said to me, "Son
> of man, eat this scroll that I give you and fill your stomach with
> it." Then I ate it; and it was in my mouth as sweet as honey
> (3:1-3).

Having had the divine message, or the Word of God, placed
directly in his mouth, the "ordination" experience was
surrounded with a series of visions and revelations that laid
out the task in which the new prophet was to engage
(1:4—5:17), the central theme of which was the proclamation of impending doom for his compatriots. Time and again

Ezekiel was told by God to confront his people with their ominous future. Though the specific oracles varied in their individual content, the basic thrust of what was to occur usually was the same. God was going to punish the nation with pestilence, famine, and sword (6:12; 6:11-12). The Lord was going to "bring the worst of the nations to take possession of their houses . . ." (7:24). War was going to rage between Babylon and Judah in Jerusalem with Yahweh as the divine instigator for the conflict (21:22; 23:22-29). As the capstone for their punishment the Lord, not the Babylonians whom he would engage as his human agents, was going to bring desolation to the land (15:8), scattering his people among the nation and driving them into foreign lands (22:15). Such all-inclusive judgment, Ezekiel was convinced, would be absolute and merciless in its fury:

> They have blown the trumpet and made all ready; but none goes to battle, for my wrath is upon all their multitude. The sword is without, pestilence and famine are within; he that is in the field dies by the sword; and him that is in the city famine and pestilence devour. And if any survivors escape, they will be on the mountains, like doves of the valleys, all of them moaning . . . (7:14-16).

The reason for the doom and its attendant suffering which Ezekiel was commissioned by God to proclaim was that the people of Israel had broken the covenant which the Lord had made with them at their beginnings as a nation!

> Therefore thus says the Lord God: As I live, surely my oath which he despised, and my covenant which he broke, I will requite upon his head (17:19).

This prophecy, though spoken to the king, is characteristic of the general tone and basis for the prophet's charges against the nation as a whole. Disregard for the Lord of the covenant, something demanded by the first commandment given in the bond at Sinai, linked with continual provocations and violations of their relationships with Him and each other, provided the abrasive that ultimately raised the divine wrath against the people of Judah. The nation had become a band of rebels who had revolted against the God to whom they

once had made their ultimate commitment of loyalty and
love. The moral signs of such rebelliousness soon had infected
every area of life. Theft, murder, broken Sabbaths, falsehood,
oppression of resident aliens—all were prevalent in the land
(22:24-29). Such antics had been prohibited strictly and
specifically in the covenant God had made with his people
when he led them out of Egyptian bondage. Added to these
acts of moral corruption, other signs of the nation's sins were
evident everywhere. Parents were being treated with con-
tempt, adultery was rampant, bribes were becoming commonplace in the courts and government, and extortion was
one of the signs of the times (22:6-12). What was as shocking
as the long catalog of sins infecting society was the fact that
the corruption was so complete and so widespread. So totally
debauched and lawless had the people become that Ezekiel
could not find a single righteous person anywhere among the
populace (22:30).

The brokenness of their relationship with God was
demonstrated by the people not only in the moral sphere,
but in their cultic or worship activities as well. Having cast
off any divinely set standards for their personal behavior, the
floodgates were opened for additional outrages of God in this
realm too. Idols were worshiped in the precincts of the house
of the Lord in Jerusalem itself (8:10). Images to the sun, an
object of worship in Egypt, being venerated by the populace,
the setting up of altars to various other alien deities "on
every high hill" and "under every green tree" (6:1-13) were
common occurrences.

While Israelite prophets in other periods of their history
saw similar corruption rampant, what is unique in Ezekiel is
that idolatry and its related perversions were seen as taking
place in the *minds* of individuals as well as in the overt
actions which could be seen and experienced (14:3-5). Thus
moral and spiritual perversion were clearly seen by Ezekiel
for what they were—alienating attitudes which led people to
separate themselves from their Lord. Hence, Ezekiel became
one of the first prophets to declare that the sins of individuals, and ultimately of society, have their real source in the

inner recesses of the heart where first comes the rejection of God and his will. Once this deep personal tie is cut, and the love for and commitment to the Lord are quenched, then a whole new orientation to life is made which inevitably becomes the pattern that determines all we do and are. As Jesus was later to say to those who crowded to hear him:

> The good man out of the good treasure of his heart produces good, and the evil man out of his evil treasure produces evil; for out of the abundance of the heart his mouth speaks. (Luke 6:43-45)

Ezekiel, therefore, saw himself surrounded by people who were destroying themselves, one another, and their future as a nation by their waywardness and corruption. From the home to the marketplace, from the mind and heart to the temple worship areas, God had been shut out of the lives of his people and their bond with him had been hurled in his face. Yet, despite all that he had experienced with them, the Lord through his prophet made a fervent plea for the people to reform their lives and give themselves back to Him. Through the human mouth into which he had early placed his words, the Lord informed the recalcitrants that he would rather save than destroy them, if only they would give him the chance:

> Therefore I will judge you, O house of Israel, every one according to his ways, says the Lord God. Repent and turn from all your transgressions, lest iniquity be your ruin. Cast away from you all the transgressions which you have committed against me, and get yourselves a new heart and a new spirit! Why will you die, O house of Israel? For I have no pleasure in the death of any one, says the Lord God; so turn, and live. (18:30-32)

As so often has been the case, the fervent offer of God of salvation rather than condemnation was rejected by the persons to whom he made the plea. Having turned their backs again on the Lord, the flood of their foolishness broke in on them as the armies of Babylon swept into Judea pillaging the countryside, strewing the fields of the land with Israelite corpses, and putting the captives in the chains which had been forged by their own sins.

Viewing his prophecies as a whole, many people conclude

that Ezekiel held hardly a shred of real hope for a reversal of his nation's life-style and commitments. The situation, as he viewed it at last, was apparently hopeless! Not only had the level of degeneration reached by the people become appalling, but the people who created the situation were themselves irreversibly evil. They had "hearts of stone" (36:27), foreheads "harder than flint" (3:9), and were stubborn beyond reforming (3:7). Not only did Ezekiel seem to learn this from bitter personal experience, but apparently God had warned him of that potential from the outset of his mission:

> And he said to me, "Son of man, go, get you to the house of
> Israel, and speak my words to them. For you are not sent to a
> people of foreign speech and a hard language, but to the house of
> Israel . . . But the house of Israel will not listen to you; for they
> are not willing to listen to me; because all the house of Israel are
> of a hard forehead and of a stubborn heart." (2:3, 7)

Because Ezekiel and God saw the people reject every plea or offer made to them to reform or return to covenant-keeping, Ezekiel prophesied the coming punishment as being absolutely certain. God was going to crush the nation and carry out his threats against them, using tactics similar to those employed by mortal kings on their enemies. God, however, would accomplish with his power the added destructiveness which only divine wrath could produce.

The prophesies of such doom make several important points. The first is that the punishment which would be levied would be universal in its application. No one would be spared the anguish of the experience (7:9). Judgment would "pass through the city" and neither age nor sex would be a deterrent to its wrath. The fury with which God would act would be so intensive that "though they cry in my ears with a loud voice, I will not hear them" (8:18).

Secondly, the people would be destroyed and/or dispossessed from their cities and homes. The shrines built to foreign deities would be laid waste and left desolate (6:5-6). What would be left standing in the country after the holocaust God was going to give to "the worst of the nations" (7:24).

Thirdly, only a remnant of the nation would survive the chastisement, though not escape it, which would be made up of people "upon whom is the mark" (9:6). Such persons Ezekiel predicted would become the seed for a later restoration of the land. Even though they were to be spared, nowhere does Ezekiel say that such people would be saved because they were righteous! It was for the sake of "God's name" that they were going to survive "that they may confess all their abominations among the nations where they go" (12:16), that is, that they could act as witnesses to the cause and fact of punishment for covenant-breaking and also provide the stock which God would later use to demonstrate anew his power and authority in rebuilding his nation before all the world (14:22).

Even though Ezekiel saw only death and destruction in the immediate future of the nation, he also prophesied that ultimately God would resurrect the nation once more. Though he would have been justified in annihilating the rebels, for reasons of his own God had chosen not to do so. Instead of wiping out his people he was going to use them to demonstrate anew to the world his sovereign power. Using the handful of survivors in wondrous and new acts, God promised to rebuild a righteous nation and in the process reorient human beings and their styles of living in ways that would right the course of history.

In a series of prophesies Ezekiel depicted the return of the remnant and the resurrection of the nation. In something akin to a new Exodus experience, the survivors would be reassembled in their homeland for a new experiment. The Lord personally would seek out those who had been driven from their homeland:

> For thus says the Lord God: Behold, I, I myself will search for my sheep, and will seek them out. As a shepherd seeks out his flock when some of his sheep have been scattered abroad, so will I seek out my sheep; and I will rescue them from all places where they have been scattered on a day of clouds and thick darkness. And I will bring them out from the peoples, and gather them from the countries, and will bring them into their own land; and I will feed them on the mountains of Israel, by the fountains, and

in all the inhabited places of the country. I will feed them with good pasture, and upon the mountain heights of Israel shall be their pasture; they shall lie down in good grazing land, and on fat pastures they shall feed on the mountains of Israel. I myself will be the shepherd of my sheep, and I will make them lie down, says the Lord God. (34:11-15)

This done, God would then select one of his people to rule them. The new ruler, or shepherd, was to come from the line of David, the great king of old.

A new covenant was to be formed with the returnees, a covenant designed so that in the "new day" the human partners would never again act rebelliously toward God (36:22-32). The crucial point in the promised covenantal relationship, which would serve as the basis for the entire restoration of the nation, was that, like the New Covenant predicted by Jeremiah (Jer. 31:31-34), the nation was going to be "programmed" or "internally oriented" by God. God, indeed, was going to *force* compliance in the future with his desires for his people:

> A new heart I will *give* you, and a new spirit I *will put* within you; and I will *take out* of your flesh the heart of stone and *give* you a heart of flesh. And I *will put* my spirit within you, and *cause* you [in Hebrew, *"make* you"] to walk in my statutes and be careful to observe my ordinances. (Ezek. 36:26-27, italics added)

What is noteworthy here is that in this new covenant the human partner was going to be totally passive in the *making* of the bond, which goes against the very nature of his/her role in the other covenants God made with the nation from the time of Moses onward. In each of those covenant events the people actively participated in accepting the relationship God was offering them (see Exod. 24:3, 7; Josh. 24:16-28). In the age to come, however, the human partners were not going to act in their own behalf in forging the agreement. God was to act unilaterally, taking over his people, and in a divinely done "heart transplant," and through the insertion of his own spirit, he was going to remove the causes for human failures in the past and provide the means for preventing any more such occurrences in the future!

After this the nation literally was to be resurrected (Ezek. 37:1ff.). The "old bones" of the house of Israel would be reassembled, enfleshed, and "enspirited" anew. In a new act of creation, similar to that at the beginning of history (Gen. 2:7), the Lord would bring forth from the earth a people he would refashion, incorporating in the reworking the new elements predicted in 36:26-27. This resurrected "body" would then reside in its homeland which was to be restored and inhabited once more (36:33). There the entire nation would be reunited. Judah, which had been wrecked by Nebuchadnezzar in 587-586 B.C., and Israel, which had been destroyed by Assyria in 721 B.C., would be restored. Like "two sticks" in one hand, the two elements of God's people would exist as one unit again, as the Lord had always desired them to be (37:15-23).

When that day of restoration would come for his heirs was never clearly specified by Ezekiel. All he would say was that before it arrived a traumatic interlude lay ahead of his contemporaries. What he did know was that both judgment and mercy eventually come from the hand of the righteous and holy God he was called and enabled to serve. That assurance sustained him when all of his efforts to change the course of national events proved to be futile.

9 THE PROPHETS FOR TODAY

Having looked at seven great prophets and the words and understandings of life and God they passed on to subsequent generations, the question remains, What ongoing value do they have for us? If their messages had been pertinent only to their own generation we probably would never have known that they even lived. But because hundreds of millions of people who were born long after these great spokesmen of the Lord died have had their preaching and insights reach deeply into their times, trials, and aspirations, the records of their sermons and oracles have remained alive and active to our day. Why?

For one thing, these great prophets have shown themselves to be perceptive evaluators of existence as it really is. All of them saw and reported life and people "in the raw," as it were, putting their fingers on issues that are both universal and apparently everlasting in their scope and duration. When it came to describing the problems of individuals and society, they fixed their focus on those dimensions of living that still touch all of our lives. People's inhumanity to people, the running roughshod over each other's dignity and rights, seem always to be with us. If you simply change the clothes, speech, and geographical settings of the people involved, the society and happenings the prophets described could well be the ones which are still bending our nation and our lives out of shape!

The denial of rights to minorities, be they women, people of color and race other than our own, or the economically weak and oppressed, is a major tragedy with which we are still struggling in this day and age. The subversion and misuse of legal systems, so that Justice seems to keep at least one eye open as she manipulates the scales, is something we read about in our daily newspapers, as well as in the books of these prophets. The violent use of power and wealth are still racking our country in particular and the world in general. The shattering experience these ministers of God had in struggling with such issues makes the prophets and their works as up-to-date as tomorrow evening's newscast.

Another reason these prophets remain important for us is that they give us keys to living life as God intended it to be lived. They pinpoint for us justice, righteousness, truth, and continuing love as the bases upon which we must build our moral structures if *shalom* is ever to be realized. Although we all long for the latter, the prophets remind us that there are no easy answers to its achievement. Life is complex, and to bring wholeness and true prosperity to it is not something that can be done simply or without sacrifice and discipline by those who desire it. Moses, Isaiah, Hosea, Amos, Micah, Jeremiah, and Ezekiel all understood that. When they called their contemporaries to live out the handful of values God had shown them in the words of life we call the commandments, they had no illusions about that occurring without every person involved giving up substantial parts of himself or herself in the process. They learned through *experience* that if everyone involved seeks only his or her own gratification then chaos and pain are the inevitable results for the entire social order. The family, community, and entire nation will collapse under the weight of the oppression such life-styles produce. The only real path to true community is reached through a morality that involves self-giving and discipline in a goal beyond immediate gratification. It involves a life-style that has at its very heart the preservation of the worth and dignity of *all* human beings, and the willingness to give *every* person his or her due.   That is why such words as *mishpat*, "to deal evenhandedly," *zanah*, "to keep in step with God," and *hesed*, "a love and respect for each other that hangs in there through good times and bad" are terms that keep reappearing throughout the prophetic books. While they are hard things to implement, as anyone who has ever tried to

live them out has learned, without them individuals and
society ultimately are doomed. We who are seeking today to
build a world where we can stop devouring one another can
find in these perceptive persons from the past the basic build-
ing blocks we too must employ if ever we are to make that
dream become a reality. The prophets do us a service by
making us realize that such a goal is painfully hard, though
with God's help possible, to achieve.

All around us these days are those who seek easy and
quick solutions to massive and difficult problems. Whether it
is new-style hawkers and peddlers of superhuman potential
programs that see nothing as being beyond our individual and
corporate powers to produce, even a twenty-first version of
Camelot, or splinter religious groups, garbing themselves in
white robes and setting up camp on a mountain slope proclaiming that God is going to descend on January 12 and
through them set up a new "government of righteousness"
which will reestablish Eden by Easter Sunday, the quick and
easy way out of our dilemmas is offered or at least longed
for! The "reality therapy" of the prophets continually shakes
us back to our senses when such appeals start becoming
attractive. Seeing history with clear eyes, evaluating people as
they are and knowing God as he is, their diagnosis and
prognosis, while sometimes disturbing, have such a ring of
authenticity about them that they make it impossible for us
to disregard them even when we would rather float off into
fantasy.

Heaven knows, as well as we do, that we have usually
failed to fully act out what these prophets have proclaimed
for our own renewal as persons and as a world community!
We have haggled with, sometimes denied or tried to shunt
aside, the convictions they were inspired to lay out for us.
Still, the accuracy and depth of the prophetic indictments
have penetrated the centuries, lodging as firmly in our consciences as a burr clings to the coat of a dog. That is one of
the reasons why after nearly three millenniums the prophets
are still with us in our generation.

What also has kept the prophets and their preaching alive

for twenty-five centuries and more is the hope they saw for
new tomorrows even when the lives of individuals and
nations were apparently hopelessly corrupt. One of the hallmarks of each of their ministries was their confidence in the
potential for change for every human being. No matter how
sordid were the persons to whom they came to preach, or
how frequently their messages seemed to fall on stopped-up
ears, they doggedly clung to the conviction that the people
they addressed had the power to be better, if they chose to
be so. Without such a conviction the preaching of the
prophets would have been a farce. Their challenge to their
countrymen to give up their sins, and their threatening them
with punishment if they refused, was based on a positive
anthropology. That is, to make such an appeal they had to be
working on the assumption that the ones they challenged
could do what the prophets were asking of them.

When Moses, Isaiah, Hosea, Amos, Micah, Jeremiah, and
Ezekiel thundered to their countrymen that the Lord was
demanding that they turn from their idolatry, adultery, theft,
lying, and murder, both they and the Lord seriously expected
them to meet those demands. As pointed out in chapter 2,
the covenant God made with Israel had imbedded in it the
assumption that the life-style outlined in the commandments
it incorporated could, in fact, be enfleshed by the human
partners of the Lord in that pact. Threats of punishment for
failure to live out these priorities were included in the provisions themselves (see Exod. 20:5-6; 12). It was precisely
because the people had the potential to use these principles
to shape their behavior that the Lord promised punishment
should they be ignored. Even Jesus later was to base his
teachings on much the same faith in the people he met. His
great commandment that the disciples love one another as he
had loved them (John 15:12) demonstrated his belief that his
friends were capable of a more positive style of living than
they themselves may ever have imagined!

In a world where so much is said and done that undercuts
a sense of positive potential in human beings, the prophetic
faith in our power "to become" is *good news*, even if it

frequently is voiced side-by-side with their critique of sinful situations and people. They continually kept in mind the fact that God had built into each human being the potential to love and serve and to live creatively with others of his/her kind. That potential was a gift from our gracious Creator at the time the race began. Though often ignored and subverted, that divine gift remained available for people to tap. That is one of the reasons the prophets continued to preach about the chance for renewal being offered by God against apparently insurmountable odds.

That faith kept the prophets going back time and time again to plead with their compatriots to reverse the trends of their lives and reshape their world. That persistent affirmation still touches a responsive chord in people who wish to believe that they and their colleagues can fashion a tomorrow better than their yesterdays.

Moreover, the prophets were able to hold out a hope for the reconstruction of even corrupt nations. No matter how bleak the past was for a people or a social order a new start was possible for both. Even when they met personally with hate and rejection, all of these prophets had as their ultimate word that God would renew his people. That held true even when the entire social structure seemed ready to collapse around them. Beyond the threats for chastisement, God's continuing promise was heard that he would not remain angry forever. Corruption could apparently be holding the day, and sin be pervading every element of society from top to bottom, and yet the prophets stood firm in the conviction that the world they saw could be renewed. Pain, suffering, isolation, and destruction might well be part of that rebirth. Still, faith in the willingness and power of God to accomplish his purposes was something they never gave up.

The prophets never doubted either the existence of God or the absolute reliability of his word! They had met him *personally* in their own lives, and had *experienced* the results of his power. Since he continued to be present and active in his world, working with it with intensity and compassion, they remained convinced that the Lord would never abandon it in any ultimate sense. Regardless of how out of kilter human beings might knock it with their antics, the day would come when the Lord would reshape and refashion the world anew. That allowed the prophets to hope for the coming of a new era even while foreign armies were marching toward their borders to devastate their country.

For oppressed, hurt, lonely, worn out, frustrated, and frantic people, the prophets' belief in the coming of a new era was good news indeed. It kept them alive, waiting and believing in times of personal and national calamity. It was "good news," the gospel, that buoyed them up when life seemed out of control and they appeared helpless.

Moses, Isaiah, Hosea, Amos, Micah, Jeremiah, and Ezekiel all caught the glimpse into the future that helped them see light at the end of the tunnel of despair. They were able to do the same for the generations that followed theirs which were confronted with their own complex of problems seemingly beyond any possibility of solution. What is even more pertinent is that they can provide *us* with a faith and encouragement to move forward to a personal and collective renewal, knowing that with the help of God a new day may be dawning, beginning *now*!

FOR FURTHER READING

For those who would like to delve more fully into the prophets covered in this book the following resources should prove to be helpful. While a few of them are somewhat technical works, they are the products of good scholars who write in a way that laypersons can understand.

1. Prophecy—"The Word of the Lord Came . . ."
   Bewer, J. A. *The Prophets in the King James Version, with Introduction and Critical Notes.* New York: Harper, 1949.
   Buber, M. *The Prophetic Faith.* New York: Harper, 1967.
   Harrelson, W. *Interpreting the Old Testament.* New York: Holt, Rinehart, & Winston, 1964.
   Kuhl, C. *The Prophets of Israel.* Richmond: John Knox Press, 1960.

2. Moses: Covenant
   Albright, W. F. *The Biblical Period from Abraham to Ezra.* New York: Harper & Row, 1963.
   Buber, M. *Moses: The Revelation and the Covenant.* New York: Harper, 1958.
   Hillers, D. *Covenant: The History of a Biblical Idea.* Baltimore: Johns Hopkins Press, 1969.
   Seilhamer, F. *And God Spoke.* Lima: C.C.S., 1971.

3. Isaiah: Sin and Restoration
   Isaiah: A New Translation. Philadelphia: Jewish Publication Society, 1973.
   Kaiser, O. *Isaiah 1-39: A Commentary.* 2 vols. Philadelphia: Westminster Press. 1972-74.
   Smith, G. A. *The Book of Isaiah.* 2 vols. London: Hodder & Stoughton, 1927.
   Wright, G. E. *The Book of Isaiah.* Vol. 11. Layman's Bible Commentary. Richmond: John Knox Press, 1964.

4. Hosea: Forgiveness
   Mays, J. L. *Hosea: A Commentary.* Philadelphia: S.C.M. Press, 1969.
   Myers, J. M. *Hosea—Jonah.* Vol. 14. Layman's Bible Commentary. Richmond: John Knox Press, 1959.
   Taylor, J. B. *The Minor Prophets.* Grand Rapids: Eerdmans, 1970.

Wolf, H. W. *Hosea: A Critical and Historical Commentary on the Bible*. Philadelphia: Fortress Press, 1974.

5. **Amos: Judgment, Justice, and Renewal**
   Garland, D. D. *Amos: A Study Guide Commentary*. Grand Rapids: Zondervan Publishing House, 1973.
   Mays, J. L. *Amos: A Commentary*. Philadelphia: S.C.M. Press, 1969.
   Ward, J. M. *Amos and Isaiah: Prophets of the Word of God*. Nashville: Abingdon Press, 1969.

6. **Micah: Righteousness and Obedience**
   Buttrick, G. A. et al. *Lamentations, Ezekiel, Daniel and the Twelve Prophets*. Vol. 6. Interpreter's Bible. Nashville: Abingdon Press, 1956.
   Gailey, J. H. *Micah—Malachi*. Vol. 15. Layman's Bible Commentary. Richmond: John Knox Press, 1974.
   Smith, J. M. et al. *A Critical and Exegetical Commentary on Micah, Zephaniah, Nahum, Habakkuk, Obadiah, and Joel*. New York: Scribner's, 1911.

7. **Jeremiah: Salvation and Faithfulness**
   Blank, S. *Jeremiah: Man and Prophet*. Cincinnati: Hebrew Union College Press, 1961.
   Hyatt, J. P. *Jeremiah: Prophet of Courage and Hope*. Nashville: Abingdon Press, 1958.
   Kuist, H. T. *Jeremiah—Lamentations*. Vol. 12. Layman's Bible Commentary. Richmond: John Knox Press, 1960.
   Skinner, J. *Prophecy and Religion: Studies in the Life of Jeremiah*. Cambridge: The University Press, 1926.

8. **Ezekiel: Punishment and Resurrection**
   Eichrodt, W. *Ezekiel: A Commentary*. Philadelphia: S.C.M. Press, 1970.
   Howie, C. G. *Ezekiel—Daniel*. Vol. 13. Layman's Bible Commentary. Richmond: John Knox Press, 1961.
   Stalker, D. M. *Ezekiel*. London: S.C.M. Press, 1968.